Carol Ann George Phd

Book Design: : Jennifer McVeigh, Aztec Printing & Design
Editing: Sophie Bellamy
Second Edition: October 2019

Acknowledgments

I would like to acknowledge the marvelous talent that collectively participated in this project, bringing together invaluable expertise, teamwork, spirit, energy, and beaming personalities. It was that sincere collective effort of this multinational team that has brought this project to life.

I want to thank Lois Hoffman, from the "Happy Self-publisher" in Delaware, the U.S. who persuaded me to bring emotion and a personal touch to the manuscript. Sincere thanks to Sophie Bellamy, a master copywriter and editor from England, who took on a virgin project and patiently made sense of it all, professionally and skilfully preparing the first edition. I thank Marymar Castro from Hidalgo, Mexico, an extremely talented graphic artist and reviewer. I also want to thank Jennifer McVeigh, from Aztec Publishers in Delaware, U.S. for the branding, and cover of the second edition. Everyone involved graciously listened and targeted my personal vision of all aspects of this very special project as I documented my own bilingual journey and invited those aspiring to finally speak Spanish to explore this approach to reach their Spanish language goals.

I thank so many countless students of Spanish throughout the years whose extreme commitment and motivation to learn fired my creativity in developing an alternative and what I believe to be, an effective approach to Spanish language learning. I want to thank Alan Spiro who the past three years, has contracted me for spoken Spanish training, allowing me to refine the early versions of Sandwich Spanish. His valuable experience and insightful feedback have played an significant role in the fine tuning of the final manuscript.

With boundless affection, I say thank you to my immense extended family, and my, dear friends all over the world, many who speak a variety of world languages other than English. Thank you all for listening, for a lifetime of loving support and affection, and for all the wonderful, sweet memories at every turn! I am eternally grateful for all of you,

Love and peace.
Carol Ann George PhD

Dedication

For Samira
My daughter, my love, and a native Spanish speaker.

At age five I overheard her telling someone at school, *"Mi papa y yo somos Mexicanos. Pero, mi mama es gringa."* This means *"my dad and I are Mexican. But my mom is American."*

I imagine that this is how she reckoned with my Spanish journey. At this young age, she had proudly articulated her identity as a Mexican, grounded in her first language. She heard it in her community and school and had already figured out that language has something to do with ethnic identity.

And she was only five!

In Loving Memory

My parents, Maud and Cecilia.

My brother Thomas and sister Elizabeth.

*Their immeasurable love, the experiences of our village,
the sacrifices of our tribe.*

My Story

An Unexpected Journey to Becoming Bilingual

I think it was destiny for me to become bilingual in Spanish and English. I grew up hearing Arabic, the language of my parents, close relatives, and the numerous families that came from our village and settled in Uniontown, Pennsylvania. Hearing the language daily and singing Arabic and Aramaic songs in the Maronite church, I developed an ear for listening and mimicking sounds that were very similar to Spanish. Rolling the r and pronouncing words with sounds produced far back in the throat seemed to come naturally to me.

Although English was my native language, I was able to thrive in our close-knit, bilingual, Lebanese community with extended family on my doorstep who spoke our native language. It was as if we were literally mirroring our home village of Abdelli, in North Lebanon. Each day, we were gifted with the melodic sounds of Arabic music, the daily conversations of our elderly speaking Arabic as they played cards under the grape vines, various dialects of Arabic music on the radio (my father was the DJ), and frequent religious and social gatherings with our beloved church at the center of our social lives. This environment represented our ethnic identity, as we indulged in the familiar sounds of the language and its significance to our culture. Truly, this was the beginning of my passionate love affair with languages. It was in my blood and in my soul! I have no doubt that it was my ethnic beginnings that seeded and nurtured my intense awareness of the tremendous power of language.

When I was in the 3rd grade, our local school piloted a Spanish program for elementary students. As a participant, I was invited to the local university to demonstrate its effectiveness. At the time, I had no idea what was happening, but now I know it was because I had responded so well to Spanish instruction. This was my first encounter with Spanish, and I loved it! I was excited, and never forgot how I felt in this dynamic language class with Mrs. Hull! Her spoken methods and positive energy were unforgettable.

In junior and senior high school, I continued studying Spanish, schlepping through the "audio-lingual" method that we all know so well. Everyone remembers the rote learning and repetition, grammar, and tests, right? We all do, but we never really learned how to create real conversations. This method was the trend at that time in schools, typically offering students the choice among French, Spanish, or German: all of which used the same, stilted method of instruction. Despite two to three years of study, most of us did not learn how to speak beyond a few basic phrases, at best.

After high school, I traveled to Lebanon for six months with my aunt Zahiah to build a school in Abdelli, our village, fulfilling my uncle's last wish. There I was able to practice Arabic and learn about my ethnic roots and our ancient culture. Stepping foot on Lebanese soil was a life-changing experience for me and what I would later realize was the profound experience that defined my lifelong relationship and passion for languages and cultures.

When I returned to the U.S., I entered Niagara County Community College, then transferred to SUNY Buffalo. There, I majored in linguistics and continued my fascination studying both Arabic and Spanish, exploring their roles in permeating cultural behaviors and norms worldwide.

At this point, unfortunately, I was still learning more *about* both languages, rather than acquiring *speaking skills* that matched the many years I had spent studying them. While it was quite interesting information, my language skills did not progress much. Yet, little did I know that things were about to change considerably.

In my junior year of college, I met my husband, Octavio who had come from Mexico to study English at the Intensive English Language Institute at SUNY Buffalo. He was already an engineer at age 20 since he started college at 15. We courted and married two years later, and after one year of working with Carborundum as an engineer, and both having completed our master's degrees, we were transferred to the Latin American operation in Toluca, Mexico. This is finally where the Spanish magic was destined to transpire.

Once in Toluca, home to the *Nevada de Toluca*, a snow-capped volcano, my Spanish immersion experience began. In just under eight months, I was able to claim a reasonable level of bilingualism. With my husband off to work, I had time to mingle in the community and focus on really learning Spanish. After starting out with a repertoire of *"hola, ¿cómo estás?"*, an initial greeting, I was beginning to reach a comfortable level of communication. I was speaking with ease and confidence, which allowed me to succeed in getting most of my needs met.

As I began to speak Spanish more fluently, I began to feel at home in my new country. I continuously practiced by watching a famous Mexican soap opera, or *novela*, 'De Pura Sangre'. My motivation also enticed me to ask questions on my visits to the open-air markets, or *mercados sobre ruedas*. A grand impetus in acquiring Spanish was when I began working for ITESM, as Director of English, where I learned academic Spanish for teaching, interacting with students and colleagues. I also spent time using Spanish to interact in correspondence. After eight months, I had become relatively fluent in academic Spanish, and since that initial push, I have steadily continued to add words, and expressions to my inventory.

From Toluca, we moved north to Chihuahua, a large industrial city where more opportunities were brewing. There, I continued to improve my own Spanish. As it were, I was also in the right place at the right time: the dawn of the North American Free Trade Agreement (NAFTA). After several requests for language services from international companies establishing operations in Mexico, I followed my path and passion and opened an adult language institute. Instituto Lingua Franca supported industry professionals from all over the world in English, Spanish, and bi-cultural training. This opportunity provided a platform for me to share my language learning expertise with professionals needing training for positions in bi-national manufacturing. After 30 years, the institute still offers language training and other services to international professionals in the city.

Mexico was the turning point for my language learning. I will always be deeply grateful for this unique, unexpected, and life-changing experience. Becoming bilingual in Spanish had afforded me countless opportunities, both professionally and personally, to engage with amazing people in the most interesting settings. Not only had I learned a second language, but as an entrepreneur, I was able to build on business skills that would later serve me in higher education and beyond.

What was to come next can only be described as fate. The next chapter of my journey came about **because** of my bilingual skills in Spanish. As I sought to pursue a PhD, I was awarded a full scholarship as a research fellow in Foreign and Second Language Education. In part, I can attribute this opportunity to a bilingual requirement of the program which focused on bilingual education and language learning. This achievement would come to enhance my professional dossier, adding to my living and working abroad. It would launch me on a new and exciting career path as a tenured professor in higher education, reaching out to share my collective gifts with students, colleagues, and the community.

Looking back, I reflect on what began back in the third grade in that experimental Spanish class, and how my journey came to fruition by way of a lifetime of unexpected endeavors, opportunities and fortunate timing. Living in Mexico and learning the language while experiencing the culture was an immeasurable gift. I continue to be in love with *mi querida México* (my dear Mexico) and its people, and their warm culture, and I hope my story can inspire you to travel, enjoy languages and cultures, and seek out the rich, loving experiences that are waiting for you around the world!

My Life's Passion

My life's passion and curiosity have always been foreign languages and the cultures that are transmitted through them. I care about the human connection through spirit and energy, using language to bring everyone to an understanding with great passion and compassion. I care about food as my medicine, relationships that nurture, and life that is full and joyful.

My lifelong relationship with languages has led me to intellectual pursuits of their power, travel to faraway places and memories of sounds, smells, and sights that I can never erase from my person. It has allowed me to touch countless human beings through instruction, and savor their unique cultures through food, dress, political views, and social norms. Like no other relationship in my life, I have come to grow old with them, watched their ebb and flow, and have brought them to a place that is settled and calm.

Languages and I are best friends for life, and I am forever grateful for their role in making me who I have become as I journey through the years. I was raised in a home where my parents and members of the community spoke Arabic and lived in Mexico where I acquired the Spanish language. Throughout life, I was continuously exposed to cultural aspects of my ethnic heritage, and for many years, the culture of Mexico. Multilingualism and multiculturalism were always part of who I was, and to this day, they continue to define my essence.

I was once told by a professor that I am what is called a "talented language learner" since I was able to learn Spanish as a near-native speaker even though English is my first language. I am fortunate to have been born with such a gift, and I am eager to share my language skills with the world!

Speaking Spanish As A Foreign Language

I understand how intimidating it can be to talk to a native speaker in a language that is not your own. I had that experience living in Mexico as an expat and as a wife of a national, and I remember the frustration and the utter urgency to learn to speak and understand what was going on in my world.

For this reason, I believe that the *Sandwich Spanish IS Painless Spanish* approach is the best way to learn to speak in a short time and to retain the language as one builds on it over time. Real learning comes from the purpose to communicate, to be understood and get our everyday needs met.

The framework of this book highlights a real need for speaking Spanish. It starts by electing a 'pivot', or key phrase that can be used " on call" in several, diverse settings. Then relevant words are presented as well as information on cultural cues. What ultimately strengthens this entire process is the firm acquisition of five clear vowels that always sound the same (and are the heart of any word in Spanish) and the consonants, which are mostly the same as English with only 12 exceptions. All together these elements allow us to begin to feel confident and at ease to articulate any sentence in Spanish. By pivoting, practicing, and accepting the language as it is, any need is fulfilled, regardless of what we know about the grammar rules! The process is streamlined and logical from the start. Isn't that what we are all looking for?

We have seen time and time again that learning about the language through grammar rules or memorization simply does not make us functional Spanish speakers. Since language is social and learned through socialization, we must have contact with the language we intend to learn. Therefore, it is imperative that we learn to use the language with a meaningful purpose, relevant to our real-life needs to communicate in real-life situations.

Sandwich Spanish will take you to that place!

Preface

This is Not a Typical Textbook

When we decide to leave home and migrate to another country for any reason, it is always a good act of faith and cordiality to learn a basic level of the native language. I believe this makes us good guests! Since language and culture are inherently linked, it is inevitable that when we learn the host language, we become a member of the community. We gain the ability to become a new carrier/messenger of the host culture, a vested citizen, and ultimately, a loyal friend. This book is written with this perspective in mind. As expats, retirees, transplants, digital nomads, etc., it is both our responsibility and desire to learn the host language and participate in our new community as members rather than as sojourners or vacationers.

Sandwich Spanish IS Painless Spanish was created with the intention to create a handbook for anyone wishing to learn spoken Spanish at a basic level. Expressions were carefully selected for their frequent usage, their potential to serve the speaker in diverse situations, and their ability to create space for expanding their usage and utility when needed. Common, vital elements needed to create real Spanish include words, sounds, and common expressions, also adding a cultural cue to complete the communication. This approach offers a practical point of departure as a foundation for building upon anyone's Spanish speaking skills at any age, regardless of their motivation for wanting to learn.

This book is not intended to be a comprehensive academic textbook. It is intentionally not grammar driven, and typical grammar terms are not used in explanations, examples, nor in practice. In addition, external resources are not referenced, except for a list of recommended Spanish resources that could provide support for further Spanish language growth. There are no traditional grammar explanations: just an offering of what is needed to get needs and desires met in Spanish.

Hopefully, this approach will move your skills far past *"hola, ¿cómo estás?"* and you will find yourself engaged in meaningful conversations in Spanish. For me, it opened doors to exciting opportunities and lifelong friendships! I am grateful and excited to share this opportunity with you as you embark on your bilingual journey!

Introduction

Welcome to Sandwich Spanish

Almost everyone I meet these days tells me they wish they could speak Spanish. They have tried high school and college courses, online resources, apps, podcasts, webinars, etc. but still have not been able to speak much when traveling abroad or speaking to friends, workmates or employees. Usually, they say that they have had enough of grammar, high school Spanish, and online 'quick fixes', and they are frustrated that they never really learned to speak Spanish-to create their own sentences and express themselves. If this is you, then this book will be just the thing to take you above and beyond what you have always wanted... **to speak and understand real Spanish!**

Sandwich Spanish provides the mantle to focus on building spoken Spanish skills that work. It uses fundamental pivots, or 'common basic phrases', that add to your creative ability to communicate. They elevate your skills to a higher level of communication, and you will learn to interact like a native in both the language and the culture.

"Topic bundles" are at the heart of *Sandwich Spanish*. They identify the **purpose** of the conversation by pinpointing **the exact language need** from the infinite possibilities that exist in all languages. They also pinpoint the most frequent language functions found in personal, social, and professional settings, such as making small talk with neighbors, dining out, and using public transportation. Added to that are 'relevant' terms that support your need for using Spanish and allow you to speak on the spot.

Instead of grammar rules, these topic bundles give you the most used, most common 'action forms' that are practical and easy to learn. **You only learn what you need!** You are not learning **about** the language, memorizing verb conjugations you will never use (nor remember anyway): you are learning to use Spanish that will allow you to function in diverse social settings!

This is not your high school Spanish class!

Sandwich Spanish will have you speaking and understanding Spanish with ease, using native-like pronunciation, and demonstrating culturally appropriate behaviors. You will be ready to take that vacation or live and thrive among the world's Spanish speaking societies!

Sandwich Spanish will take you all the way!

You might be wondering, why the focus on culture? Manners are extremely important throughout the world, but especially in Spanish speaking countries. Knowing how to begin and end a conversation in Spanish is just as important as the primary message that you wish to convey. The "three-part formula" in *Sandwich Spanish* allows you to get the attention of the listener, state what your intention or purpose is, and then politely close the interaction in a culturally appropriate manner. Their response to your request will be met with pleasure as you display your native-like skills and sensitivity to the culture.

Sandwich Spanish was created to guide you, the speaker, into the conversation and build your self-confidence which is the key element in learning any skill- Especially communicating in Spanish! The carpenter, the neighbor, the waitress, and the taxi driver will all be impressed and will tend to prolong the communication, giving you the continued opportunity for real practice to improve your skills. You will be constantly motivated as you experience the feeling of success when you communicate in Spanish! Whether you are in a Spanish-speaking country for a month, six months, or even several years, you will show your hosts that you care enough to make the effort to speak their native tongue-Spanish.

Finally, you made it!

How To Use This Book

You are about to embark on your **last** journey to learning Spanish, but first, it is important to understand how to get the most from this book and truly make it your reality.

First, for optimal, effective, and lasting results, it is essential to **master the information in the introduction.** This covers everything you need to speak or understand Spanish and explains what is expected of you as you embark on this journey. A realistic investment of **time** to learn, a **commitment** to yourself, and **acceptance of the language** ALL contribute to your effort to make a difference once and for all! You will save time and energy if you accept Spanish as it is, without comparing it to English. It is its own linguistic system, as is any language. So, accepting it 'as is' is key.

Next, focus on the key facts of language learning and be aware that anyone can learn a new language. It is something truly attainable at any age! Believing this drives your learning and tears down any obstacles in your way.

As you approach the lessons, take note: the variety of topic bundles, or settings, were selected based on their **frequency of need**. How often will you come across the key phrases? How often will you need to use them? Will it be to speak to repair personnel, or to a waiter? The good news is that these topic bundles can be learned by investing little time, but they will come in handy quite often as you will use their phrases and words repeatedly in a variety of contexts. In time, they will become automatic and simply roll off your tongue! Isn't that the idea? You will get a lot of bang for your buck: one frequently used phrase, customized to YOUR needs, can serve you over and over again.

If you really want your Spanish to sound native, I strongly suggest you first spend the necessary time focusing particularly on the sounds of the **vowels and consonants.** This is what will most lead to near-native pronunciation that listeners will appreciate. They won't hear 'gringo Spanish', but a smooth, accurate rendition of their language. Mastering the sounds will boost your confidence and competence as a Spanish speaker. I cannot stress how important this is since it affects your communication in speaking and listening as well as your self-confidence and drive to continue your Spanish journey. To reach your goal, it is important to consistently continue your journey to becoming bilingual, a skill that takes time and again, contact with the language.

The simplicity of only mastering five vowel sounds and their purity makes it easy to then focus on the similar sounds of the consonants. Further, you will become aware of the exceptions, or sounds that differ in English, including that 'H' is always silent, and 'LL' is always 'Y'. We come to understand and accept that learning the sounds and mastering their production leads us to speak Spanish with an accent that approaches a native speaker! Bravo!

English and Spanish are brothers. Not twins, but brothers. English acquired 50% of the Latin language due to the Norman conquest, (the French) in England around 1066. During this time, the English language underwent many important linguistic changes that affect how we speak English today. Since Spanish comes from Latin, and English acquired 50% of French, also from Latin, you are already familiar with 50% of the Spanish language. You can use this likeness to successfully guess the meanings of many words you hear or find the words you need to express yourself in spoken Spanish.

These "cognates" are words that have the same origin and look alike or similar. Words like "secretary" and "*secretaria*", "number" and "*número*", and "mountain" and "*montaña*" give you the advantage of using 50% of your own vocabulary to make sentences in Spanish. Then, leaving you to only learn the other 50%. Isn't this a wonderful benefit? Your awareness and acceptance of this allow you to focus less on learning random words and more on combining words you know with phrases in this book to create real, valuable Spanish. So, don't be afraid to guess! Chances are, it will be the right word in Spanish! If it sounds good in English, it probably sounds good in Spanish!

While Spanish dialects differ among Spain, the U.S., Mexico, Central and South America, the expressions and words presented here are familiar to speakers we may interact with in Mexico, Central America, and South America. Although there are some linguistic differences, Iberian Spanish, or Spanish spoken in Spain is the same language, so you will be able to communicate using your new-found skills with any Spanish speaker, regardless of where they are from. It is the same language, with minimal differences in words, sounds, and structures.

On a final note, you can use this book in any order, as needed, without following a sequence. Each bundle is designed for you to communicate in Spanish to solve an immediate problem, or for any daily purpose in your life. So, ready, set, let's begin our journey to speaking Spanish!

¡Vámanos!   *Let's Go!*

Table of Contents

Unit 1

Unit 2

What Is Needed Of You

Your Commitment to Sandwich Spanish

Since learning a language is a skill that only improves with practice, it is important to acknowledge what you need before commencing your learning and promise yourself not to give up until you reach your language goals.

Do you have what you need to succeed? Let's see!

- The commitment of time and energy.

- Acceptance of the language as it is.

- Confidence in your ability to learn Spanish.

- Personal drive for self-improvement.

- Perseverance and a can-do attitude.

Consider these key points

- Adults DO learn languages with near-native fluency.

- We can only learn a language by having contact with the language.

- Children do not learn better than adults. In some cases, adults do better.

- You don't need grammar to speak Spanish. Forget it!

- English is 50% French, so you already know 50% of Spanish! These words in English come from Latin.

- One language is not harder than another.

- Spanish is phonetic, which means you say what you see! English is morphemic, which means that it's made up of units of meaning that can be spelled the same but pronounced differently. This is the reason there are no spelling bees in Spanish speaking countries!

- Language is infinite, so you must first identify your need to learn it, then focus on that for results. Saying "I want to speak Spanish" is not specific enough.

- Being bilingual is an elite skill worldwide, and monolingualism can be cured!

- The more time invested, the better your Spanish.

- The more opportunities to practice, the more you will improve! Take them!

- Only people from Spain are Spanish! Anyone who speaks Spanish has their own country and nationality. A Puerto Rican is not Spanish, but Spanish speaking!

Lastly, language is social! So only active interactions in Spanish will improve your Spanish speaking skills. Nothing else! So, be sure to take advantage of being immersed in any social setting where Spanish is spoken. It is your giant language laboratory!

The Sandwich Spanish Method

A Simple Sandwich of Communication

We all know how important it is to speak Spanish while respecting cultural norms. Therefore the 'bread' is an important part of this sandwich. It represents the cultural beginning and ending of your communication in Spanish. The "meat" represents both the forms of the language (structures), and the functions (purpose) we place between the two pieces of bread.

Written or formal Spanish is not the same as spoken Spanish. This is also true in English. Colloquial or everyday language differs in many ways. Attempting to speaking formal, or written Spanish may put off your listeners and lead you to believe that they don't understand you. Hence, you will not feel confident to practice, and without practice, you will never improve and reach your goal.

The goal of *Sandwich Spanish* is to learn to speak about frequent topics, master them, then build through pivots and frequently used words to accumulate a rich inventory you can use anytime, anywhere. This method was developed to combine the purpose for speaking Spanish to fulfill an immediate need or solve a problem, with culturally appropriate delivery. It consists of common greetings and closures (the bread) placed around the purpose to communicate (the meat). **The result is a simple sandwich of communication that sounds exactly like a native speaker: natural, easy, and inviting. If it were a sandwich, it would look like this:**

Sandwich Spanish was developed to give you more than isolated phrases that you don't know, when, or how to use. Instead, it gives you the edge to sound native-like by incorporating the three basic elements of popular conversational Spanish. Without all three, no matter how well you know rules and vocabulary, you will not have the same cultural impact when approaching a native Spanish speaker. Since language is the vehicle that transfers and transports culture and behavior, it is important to incorporate these nuances when learning Spanish or any other new language. It completes the communication and sounds familiar to native Spanish speakers. The Sandwich formula *makes sense* to them in its three parts, rather than in isolated, awkward sentences that sound stilted. Framing the purpose with appropriate greetings and leave-taking means you have the essentials for being respectful and *"educado(a)"* (polite/mannerly) in Spanish speaking societies. You are accepted with open arms into your new-found community!

Greet - Get Attention

Communicate Purpose

Appreciate - Say Goodbye

What Is In Each Topic Bundle?

An Introduction to the Topic Bundles

Living or visiting any Latin American country means you will be in touch with individuals from many colorful and friendly cultures where Spanish is the mother tongue. If you are traveling or are living in any of these countries, it makes sense that you will want to communicate with people in the most amazing and diverse settings.

A ball rolling up to you on a beach, a neighbor in need of small talk, or the desire to gratefully compliment the chef at your favorite restaurant are all messages you will want to convey in Spanish. You will want to feel part of the community by being sociable and friendly, reaching out in the language of your new home. This book was written with you in mind.

Each topic bundle begins with a specific setting that revolves around a real and frequent need to speak Spanish effectively and confidently. Each topic bundle involves the before and after expressions that go with the purpose for speaking Spanish on that topic. The top and the bottom bread of the sandwich are language standards or courtesies that are used to introduce and close your purpose. You will feel that you are repeating them over and over. Well, you are because they are culturally necessary when addressing a native speaker. The meat of your sandwich is the actual purpose and the phrase that you need to use to convey your message. All combined, they make up natural Spanish conversation.

The 'key lesson pivots' of each chapter were **carefully selected to give you the most frequent and useful phrases** you will need. They are enhanced by adding words and actions to create a multitude of expressions. You will learn what native speakers really use in everyday language, instead of wasting precious time learning expressions that no one ever uses! There is no need to remember grammar rules, boring verb conjugations, or a lot of other people (*yo, tú, él,* etc.). **You only learn what you need!** It is not necessary to include anyone who is not in the room! *Make sense? Of course!* Conversations typically involve you and the other person - *yo y tú!* Forget all the others for now! *Simple is always a better place to start!*

So, now you will become familiar with the Spanish sounds, (pure vowels and consonant exceptions), and you will remember that it is important to accept the language as it is. So, invest your time and energy in perfecting all the elements in each topic bundle; key lesson pivots, condiments, practice and exercises. Integrate the 'cultural cues' and the 'pronunciation tips' and you will be ready to speak Spanish confidently with warmth and ease, demonstrating your personal determination to embrace the culture, and connect with truly remarkable people!

Pronouncing Spanish Vowels

The Heart of Speaking Spanish

There are only **five predictable vowel** sounds in Spanish! How wonderfully easy is that to remember? We can divide these five vowels into two groups:

Group 1:

A is ALWAYS like 'father'.

> E.g. *plátano* = banana

But E and I are different from English.

E is ALWAYS a long A: as in 'ace' (remember the e = ace as in the ace in a deck of cards).

> E.g.   *mesa* = table

I is ALWAYS a long E: as in 'meet' (remember the I = heat).

> E.g.   *tipo* = type or kind of thing

> **Note:** The same long 'E' sound is made with the letter 'Y' when it follows the vowels 'A', 'O', and 'U'. E.g. *Muy, soy,* and *mayo.* 'Y' can be a vowel or a consonant depending on what position it is in in the word. At the end of the word, it is always 'E'.

Group 2:

O and U are always pronounced without rounding the lips at the end. They sound like English long 'O' and long 'U' but shorter. Leave your mouth open and remember there is no puff of air at the end.

> O =   E.g. *gato* (cat)
> U =   E.g. *gusto* (pleasure)

That's it! **Only five sounds to learn!** They will never change and will never leave you hanging. They are very loyal friends! **Nothing will improve your accent more than learning these five simple sounds!**

Pronouncing Spanish Consonants

Learning the Exceptions

Generally, Spanish consonants are like English consonants with **only 12 easy exceptions**. They are easy to learn and will have you speaking Spanish **like a native!**

1. **V and B are closely pronounced as 'B' in Mexico and in other Spanish speaking countries.** The lips are only slightly apart. Once you master this exception, your accent will immediately improve and sound less gringo. Although you say them the same, they are not the same in writing.

2. **D is ALWAYS pronounced 'TH'**. It is the most noticeable way to sound native and less gringo.

3. **S and Z are usually pronounced the same in Latin America as a soft 'S'.** An exception would be Spanish spoken in Spain where the 'S' sound is pronounced as 'TH' in some regions. There is no hard 'Z' in Spanish. This sound does not exist. In these examples, both words begin with the same sound, 'S'.

    E.g.   *Sano* (s) = healthy
            Zebra (s) =zebra

4. **T is not aspirated.** That is, there is no puff of air at the end.
    E.g.   time (puff of air)
            tiempo (Softer T sound with NO puff of air).
            Put your hand to your mouth to feel the difference.

5. **LL is ALWAYS 'Y'**. Just think of *'tortilla'*. It can be said as 'tor TEE ya' (enunciate the 'Y'), stressing the second syllable.

6. **H is ALWAYS silent!** Except when it is after 'C' (mucho, for example).

    E.g.   Honor = *onor* (pure o, as in 'go')

7. **G is ALWAYS soft** like 'H' before E and I.

    E.g.   *Gente* = people (G = H)
            Gigante = giant, large (G = H)

8. **G is a hard 'G'** as in English (gas) before A, O & U.

   E.g.   *Gato* = cat
   Gota = drop
   Gusto = pleasure

   Note that the same rule holds true for the letter 'C'.
   C = K after A, O & U   E.g. *Cantar, Combinar, Cumbre*
   C = S after E & I   E.g. *Centavo, Citar, cenote*

9. **J is like 'H' too**, but it is a deeper sound made far back in the throat. You can say it as 'H' using the back of your throat (think 'K' or 'G' in English).

   E.g.   *Jugo* = juice
   Juez = judge

10. **Spanish R is made with the tongue tapping** behind the back of the teeth (rolled R).

    E.g.   *Pero* = but

At the beginning of a word, (rojo), or as a double R (perro) it is the same 'rolled R', but intensified, longer, and strong! Like an airplane!

   E.g.   *Rojo* = red
   Perro = dog

So, pero and perro are not the same! Relax: it takes time to learn it well, and you are still understood!

11. **The Ñ = n + yay.** In words, it is pronounced:

    E.g.   *Mañana* - Man - ya - na = tomorrow
    Tamaño - Ta - man - yo = size

   Both consonants and vowels:

12. The combinations of two sounds as **"QUE" and "QUI" never change.**

    "Que" = Kay   *"Qui"* = Key

   Although Spanish is phonetic, these sound combinations must be learned and pronounced as they are

   E.g.   *Queso* (kay so):   cheese
   Quitar: (Key tar):   to remove, take off

No More Gringo Spanish!

Pronunciation Advice

1. When speaking Spanish, **first pick out the vowels** which are the heart of each syllable (you can't have a syllable without a vowel).

   Once you pronounce all the vowels correctly, then add in the remaining consonants.

   This helps to be sure you are including the **right number of syllables** in Spanish (if you must, count them on your hand or beat them on the table).

2. **Spanish is a consonant-vowel (CVCVCV) language** which is why it sounds so melodic to non-native speakers. So, all vowels have the same length and they all deserve your attention!

   So, if you say the vowel first and make it strong, you will be sure to have the correct rhythm, include all syllables, and be better understood. You can even clap on each vowel to bring out the sound. For example:

	Subject	Verb	Object
E.g.	*El camino*	*te lleva*	*a la playa*
	The road	takes you	to the beach

3. **There are no 'short' vowels in Spanish**, which means there are no sounds like in the words let, hat, cook, up, or not, etc. Stick to your **five loyal friends:** A, E, I, O, U. They won't let you down! They ALWAYS sound the same. They are PURE at heart!

4. **Move from the known to the unknown.** That is, try something in English first, and then move it to Spanish. Chances are, since the two languages are brothers, and both follow the same word order, you are going to say it perfectly, or at least be very close. In the following example, they are identical.

	Subject	Verb	Object
E.g.	*Juan*	*trabaja*	*en Cancún.*
	John	works	in Cancun.

5. **Cognates are words that can mean the same** and look the same in two languages because they have the same or similar origin. They are what we use to grow our vocabulary, i.e. secretaria and secretary. At times, we encounter **false cognates** which are words that trick us into thinking they are cognates with the same meaning, but they are not!

   E.g.   Actual in English = real, authentic

Actual in Spanish = current, recent, now

The good news is that cognates are still the best way to guess a new word and learning them is also important since they add to our growing inventory of words in Spanish. So, take a guess on a new word! Chances are, **it will be perfect!**

Remember that English is 50% French, and French and Spanish are both from Latin. So, it is safe to say you already know 50% of Spanish just by knowing English! How great is that!

What is important is that you TRY to speak! Use what you know. You are probably going to be right! Remember, **if it sounds good in English, it probably sounds good in Spanish!**

So, let's sum it up. What have you learned about Spanish as you embark on your last Spanish lessons?

You know the common myths regarding learning a second language, as well as the things to do to "sound" like a native speaker. And, best of all, you are familiar with the only five vowels you will ever need, and the familiar consonants with the 12 Spanish consonant exceptions. Finally, you can engage your cognate knowledge when you need to add to your growing vocabulary!

So, in any order, pick a topic you may need right now, and go!

Just remember, for native pronunciation you need:

1. The five pure vowels – A E I O U – never change.

2. The consonants that are close to or like English consonants.

3. The consonant exceptions: 12 that you must learn.

> **¡Adelante y mucha suerte!**
> *Go ahead and best of luck!*

Topic Bundle 1
Visiting a Restaurant

My story: learning food in Spanish

After a couple of months, we were still living in a hotel on our new assignment in Toluca, just outside of Mexico City. We were at a dinner with other couples from the company and after a long time of having my husband talk for me, I decided I wanted to try my hand at ordering in Spanish, so I asked the waiter to bring me a "pastel de moco" (booger cake) instead of "mocha" (chocolate cake)! Okay, it's only one letter! But I quickly realized my mistake and said, "I mean mocha!"

The laugh from that faux pas lives on even today! But isn't that part of learning a language? Trial and error? I never did live this one down! Still the best story.

Sandwich Spanish Ingredients

Visiting a Restaurant

In this chapter, you are using *Sandwich Spanish* to function in a restaurant setting. What else is more enjoyable than enjoying traditional dishes, especially in Latin America? Have a taste of your restaurant sandwich

The Bread - Step 1: Greeting

Politely get attention. Always begin with: **Buenos días, buenas tardes, or buenas noches.** *Notice that we only use "buenos" in the morning!*

Disculpa, discúlpame.	Excuse me.
Perdón, perdonáme.	Excuse me. What did you say?
Señor.	Sir, or Mr.
Señora.	Married woman.
Señorita.	Single woman, or if uncertain.
Joven (j-h).	Young man, or waiter.

The Meat - Step 2: Communicate Purpose

Things you would ask or say as you enter and are seated at a restaurant. Don't forget to add por favor to your requests!

¿Me trae el menú?	Can you bring me the menu?
¿Tiene mesa para ocho?	Do you have a table for eight?
¿Dónde está el baño/sanitario?	Where is the bathroom?
Tráigame un café.	Bring me a coffee.
Me gustaría vino tinto/blanco.	I would like red/white wine.
¿Me trae la cuenta?	Can you bring me the check?
Me gustaría una mesa para dos.	I would like a table for two.

The Bread - STEP 3: Appreciate and Depart

Things you would ask or say as you leave a restaurant. You enjoyed the food and atmosphere.

Gracias, muy amable.	Thank you. It's very kind of you.
Está bien, gracias.	It's fine, thank you.
Gracias. Muy rico.	Thank you, it (was) delicious.
¡Deliciosa (o)!	Delicious!
¡Nos encanto!	We loved it!
Gracias, que le vaya bien.	Thanks, hope all goes well for you.
Gracias, nos vemos.	Thank you, see you.
¡Bonito día, Buen día!	Have a nice day!

When you are looking for a place to eat, there are usually many delicious, fresh options. You can even order food for delivery! The main meal, or *"la comida"*, is usually later than 1 pm and lasts a couple of hours. In some places, businesses close and families and friends gather to eat together.

The *"siesta"* is usually a rest after the large meal. Later, work, business, and even classes resume until evening, and then it's time for a light supper.

These are some typical things you might say at the table:

Buen provecho.	Enjoy your meal.
Salud, amor, y dinero.	(A toast) To health, love, and money.
¡Salud!	Cheers!
Adelante.	Go ahead and begin eating.
Arriba, abajo, al centro, y pa' dentro.	A popular drinking toast: Above, below, in the middle and down the hatch (inside)

Typical breakfast – desayuno

Jugo de naranja	Orange juice
Piña, zanahoria, pepino, tomate	Pineapple, carrot, cucumber, tomato
Café Americano	Brewed coffee
Café de grano	Drip coffee, as opposed to instant

Leche de vaca, de coco, cabra	Cow's milk, coconut milk, goat's milk
Licuado de fruitas	Fruit smoothie
Licuado verde	Green smoothie
Huevo al gusto	Eggs made to order
Huevo frito, revuelto, cocido	Eggs Fried, scrambled, boiled
Frijoles fritos	Refried beans
Chilaquiles	Corn tortilla in green/red sauce
Avena o cerea	Oatmeal or cereal
Yogur con fruta	Yogurt with fruit
Pan dulce, pan blanco	Sweet bread or white bread
Pan de barra, o de caja	Sliced bread
Pico de gallo	Fresh salsa: chopped
Hotcakes y wafles	Hotcakes and waffles

Typical lunch – la comida (largest meal of the day)

Un refresco o soda	A flavored,carbonated drink or soda
Una cerveza	A beer
Una copa de vino	A stemmed glass of wine
Té helado	Iced tea
Agua en botella	Bottled water
Agua de la llave	Tap water
Agua de frutas	Water made with fresh fruit
Cortes de carnes	Cuts of meat
Pollo: rostizado/frito	Chicken roasted/fried
Cocido en mole/en adobo	Cooked in mole/adobo sauce
Mariscos	Seafood
Camarones, pulpo, pescado	Shrimp, octopus, fish
Ensalada de verdura	Vegetable salad

Lechuga romana (oreja)	Romaine lettuce
Sopa de papa	Potato soup
Sopa de tortilla, cebolla o marisco	Tortilla, onion, or seafood soup
Postre del día	Dessert of the day
Pay de manzana	Apple pie
Pastel de tres leches	Three milk cake
Una rebanada de pizza	A slice of pizza

Typical supper: la cena

Supper is usually light, but restaurants serve dinners to accommodate tourists, late-night events and dinners. It is becoming more common for many to eat large suppers, especially if they work far from home and are not able to be home for "la comida" during the day. This is especially true in larger towns and cities.

Sandwich Spanish Condiments

Spice up your Sandwich with these 'Condiments'!

Adelante	Right this way/go ahead/please begin
El menú/la carta	The menu
Con permiso	Excuse me: If you: pass by someone/leave
Pásale	Go ahead (answer to 'con permiso')
A sus órdenes	May I help you? At your service
Si, dígame	Yes, how can I help you (tell me)?
Más	More
Menos	Less
Con	With
Sin	Without
Caliente	Hot (temperature)
Picoso	Spicy (not caliente)
Aperetivo	Appetizers
Entradas	Starters
Al lado	On the side/side dish
Mariscos	Seafood
Carne	Meat
Pollo	Chicken
Verdura	Vegetables
Fruta	Fruit
Ensalada	Salad
Pan	Bread
Pan dulce	Sweet bread
Tortilla (de maíz/harina)	Tortillas (corn/flour)
Sal y pimiento	Salt and pepper

La hora feliz	Happy hour
Desayuno	Breakfast
Comida	Largest meal of the day (1 pm – 3 pm)
Cena	Supper, can be light
Bebidas	Drinks
Copa de vino	A glass of wine (stemmed glass)
Un vaso de leche	A glass of milk
Un vaso de refresco	A glass of soda
Taza de café o té	A cup of coffee or tea
Un Café	A coffee
Un trago	An alcoholic drink of any kind

Terms For Your Word Wheel

Things you would like to HAVE: Me gustaría_____.

Un café.	A cup of coffee.
Una ensalada.	A salad.
El pescado.	The fish.
Mas café.	More coffee.
Un hamburguesa.	A hamburger.
Té helado (con hielo).	Iced tea (with ice).
Un vaso de agua.	A glass of water.
Una copa de vino.	A stemmed glass of wine.
Tinto o blanco.	Red or white.

Things you would like to DO: Me gustaría_____.

Ordenar.	Order something: food, car parts, etc.
Comer carne.	Eat meat.
Pedir ayuda.	Ask for help.
Ver el menu.	See the menu.
Tomar un vino.	Drink some wine.
Invitarte a comer.	Invite you to eat.
Tomar una cerveza.	Drink a beer.
Sentarme en una mesa.	Sit at a table.

Remember! You do not need to change these words! Keep it simple! Just begin with *"me gustaría"*, and then **add the thing you want**, or the **action you want to do**. Create as many as you need. This phrase is a good friend that will go with you anywhere you need to speak Spanish!

Growing Your Sandwich Spanish

Word Wheel with Key Pivot Practice

Pivot 1: Me gustaría___. = I would like___ I would like to___.

"Me gustaría" is a very handy phrase since it is used for things and actions in a variety of settings. If you **want something**, or if you **want to do something**, you can use it. Here are examples used with things and actions. Note that you only need to use the action words that end in er, ar, and ir. Leave them alone and just add them to *"me gustaría"*.

Your turn! Practice using the center pivot to create numerous sentences in Spanish! Be creative by using everything you have learned in this lesson and beyond!

Cultural Cue: You can use *"quiero"* when ordering in a restaurant which is like saying "I want", but this may sound a bit demanding. The correct and more polite way is to say "me gustaría". It is not as assuming or direct. This pivot from your sandwich is used often and in a variety of settings!

Pivot 2: ¿Tiene___? = Do you have___.

"Tiene" means "has" or "have" and is used to ask someone if they have something. It is useful when shopping or eating out and is used frequently in conversation. **It is the same as "do you carry_____?" (As in a store merchandise).**

Your turn! Practice using the center pivot to create numerous sentences in Spanish! Be creative by using everything you have learned in this lesson and beyond!

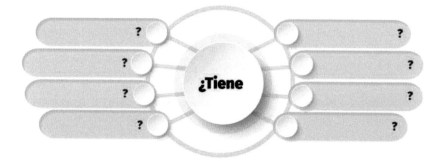

Pronunciation Tip: The sound of 'T' in Spanish is like the English 'T'. However, it has one difference: an English 'T' has a puff of air at the end and the Spanish 'T' does not. You can practice by holding your hand to your face when you say it. If there's no air, you've got it right!

Pivot 3: ¿Dónde está ____? = Where is ____?

"¿Dónde está?" is used to ask where something is. So, if you need to use the bathroom, you say, *"¿dónde está el baño?"* Only **things or living things** can follow this. Be sure you are using *"la"* and *"el"*. You can also use *"mi"* and *"tu"* when something belongs to someone. We say "where **is** the bathroom", not, "where bathroom". So, if you want to sound native-like, be sure to say one of these!

Your turn! Practice using the center pivot to create numerous sentences in Spanish! Be creative by using everything you have learned in this lesson and beyond!

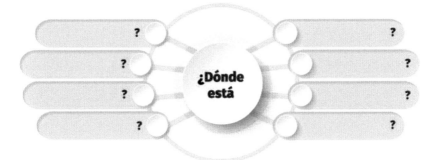

> **Pronunciation Tip:** When one word ends, and another begins with the **same vowel,** we pronounce them as ONE vowel. This means we that omit one syllable. So, *"¿dónde está?"* (four beats), sounds like *"dondesta"* (three beats). You can count it out when you say it. Don-des-ta. 1, 2, 3! Now you sound like a native speaker!

Pivot 4: Tráigame_____, por favor. = Bring m_____, please.

"Tráigame" and *"me trae"*, mean the same thing. They are frequently used to make a request or order food in a restaurant. *"Me trae"* is somewhat more formal, but both are appropriate – we will come to that next.

Your turn! Practice using the center pivot to create numerous sentences in Spanish! Be creative by using everything you have learned in this lesson and beyond!

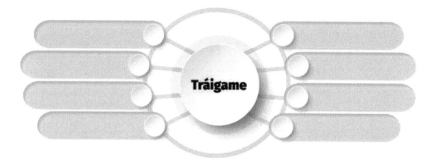

> **Pronunciation Tip:** Remember that each vowel is a syllable or a beat. So, *"tráigame"* has four beats, not three! You will say, *"tra ee ga me"* which makes four syllables. Your gringo accent is disappearing fast! *Bravo!*

Pivot 5: ¿Me trae_____? = Can you bring me_____?

"Me trae" is another way to say, "bring me_____", or "can you bring me_____?" It is more formal that *"traigame"* and is used when you want to be respectful and polite. "Me trae" is three beats: each vowel is the heart of the syllable!

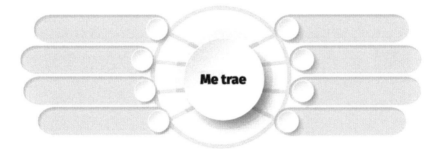

Your turn! Practice using the center pivot to create numerous sentences in Spanish! Be creative by using everything you have learned in this lesson and beyond!

Pronunciation Tip: It is important to say all the vowel sounds you see. *"Me trae"* has three vowels, not two, so be sure you are saying all three! This is what makes your accent sound native! *Bravo,* great job!

Expanding your Spanish:
More Key Pivot Practice

Use the *Spanish Sandwich* method (bread-meat-bread), the dressings, the key pivots, the sides, and all you know about the sounds to create your own sandwich. Also, use cognates, or words that come from the same origin, to recall words you already know. Bring these all together and make your own unique Spanish sandwiches!

¡Adelante! *Go ahead!*

Bread:

Meat:

Bread:

Bread:

Meat:

Bread:

Bread:

Meat:

Bread:

Bread:

Meat:

Bread:

Cultural Cue: When you walk past anyone who is eating, you say "*provecho*" or "*buen provecho*", which means "enjoy your meal" or "bon appetite!" When strangers say this to you while passing (and they will), you can respond, "*gracias, igualmente*", meaning "thank you, same to you"

Igualmente is a terrific phrase! Imagine other times you might use it! For example: "*Mucho gusto*" (nice to meet you), "*igualmente*" (same here)..

Common Restaurant Expressions

Now you can garnish your *Spanish Sandwich* by using these phrases to communicate in any restaurant setting. Use what you know about the vowels and consonants to sound like a native! Use them whenever you can!

¡Qué delicioso! ¡Muy rico!	How delicious! Very delicious! (good)
¿Qué se le ofrece?	What can I offer you? How can I serve you?
¡Es dulce!	It is sweet!
¡Es salado!	It is salty!
Tengo alergia al huevo.	I am allergic to eggs.
¿Qué recomiendas?	What do you recommend?
Soy vegetariano, soy vegan.	I am a vegetarian, I am a vegan.
Dos chelas (cheves) por favor.	Two beers, please.
¿Cuál es el plato del dia?	What is the daily special?
Mande. ¿Mande usted? (Mexico)	Excuse me? I did not hear you.
¿Quién es el chef?	Who is the chef?
Aqui esta su propina.	Here is your tip.

Cultural tip: Eating in Latin America is still seen as a shared event: one is not on the go, nor eating in the car! Dining is taken slowly with drinks, appetizers, and lots of conversation. Perhaps even music! Most believe that eating is still one of the best pleasures in life! Take it slow and enjoy! *¡Buen provecho!*

Wrap it up &
Take it To Go!

What I Can Politely Do In Native-Like Spanish:

- Secure a table for the number of people I need.

- Secure a table in the space I prefer.

- Get a menu and ask for various foods and drinks.

- Ask for the bathroom.

- Request the check.

- What else can you do?

I Am Culturally Skilled To:

Interact with others respectfully and confidently at a restaurant, including those who serve me and those I may meet.

¡Buen provecho!   Enjoy your meal!

Topic Bundle 2
Traveling by Bus or Train

My story: an immigration scare!

So, on our trial visit to Toluca, we were in Mexico City trying to board the plane back to Buffalo when we realized we did not have a passport nor papers for our daughter who was six months old! We were detained as though they thought we might be kidnapping or trafficking her! After the officials observed my interaction with her, they determined that "she does act like her mother." I certainly would hope so!

So, we were given a temporary ID for her to travel home. What a scare that was! I guess it was different times! We probably wouldn't get away with this today!

Sandwich Spanish Ingredients

Travel by Bus or Train

In this chapter, we are using *Sandwich Spanish* to function while traveling by bus, plane, or train. What else is more pleasurable and satisfying than learning to get around the local area or distant points of interest feeling safe and confident? Have a taste of your travel sandwich!

The Bread : Step 1: Greeting

Politely get attention. Always begin with: **Buenos días, buenas tardes, or buenas noches.** Notice that we only use "buenos" in the morning!

Disculpa, discúlpame.	Excuse me.
Perdón, perdonáme.	Excuse me. What did you say?
Señor.	Sir, or Mr.
Señora.	Married woman.
Señorita.	Single woman, or if uncertain.
Joven (j-h).	Young man, or waiter.

The Meat: Step 2: Communicate Purpose

Things you would like to ask while traveling.

¿Dónde está la estación del tren?	Where is the train station?
¿La estación de camiones esta lejos?	Is the bus station far?
¿Hay boletos a Mérida?	Are there tickets to Merida?
¿Cuánto cuesta el boleto?	How much does the ticket cost?
¿Me da dos, por favor?	Can you give me two, please?
?A qué hora sale?	What time does it leave?
¿A qué hora llega?	What time does it arrive?
¿Cuál asiento tengo?	What seat do I have?
¿Dónde pongo mi maleta?	Where do I put my suitcase?
¿Hay comida y aire abordo?	Is there food and air on board?

The Bread - Step 3: Appreciate And Depart

Things you would ask or say after getting help with your trip.

Gracias por su ayuda.	Thank you for your help.
Gracias, muy amable.	Thank you. It's very kind of you.
Perfecto, gracias.	Perfect, thank you.
¡Nos encantó! ¡Me encantó!	We loved it! I loved it!
Buen día, gracias.	Have a good day, thank you.

Sandwich Spanish Condiments

Spice up your Sandwich with these 'Condiments'!

Mi maleta. Mi beliz	My suitcase.
Mi equipaje	My luggage (baggage)
La ventanilla	The ticket counter
Comprar	To buy, purchase
El horario	The schedule of departures and arrivals
Un descuento	A discount
Viaje redondo	A round trip ticket
Viaje sencillo	One-way ticket
El pasillo	The aisle
La entrada	The entrance
La salida	The exit
Subir	To board, get on a bus, train, plane
Bajar	To leave, get off a bus, train, plane
El portero	Person who takes tickets/carries bags
En efectivo	Cash
Con tarjeta	With a credit card
Con débito	With a debit card

Un Recibo	A receipt
Una reservación	A reservation
Llamar a un taxi	Call a taxi
Está lejos	It is far.
Está cerca	It is nearby.

Note: when you are asking about the price of a ticket, just ask, *"¿Cuánto cuesta?"* How much does this cost? In all languages, the answer is **ALWAYS** "hiding" in the question. The answer is *"Cuesta cien pesos."* Be a good listener and you will hear the answer in the question! Then just answer with the same word used in the question.

Variations For Your Word Wheel: "Hay"

Statement singular: There is _____.

Hay café en la estación.	There is coffee in the station.
Hay tiempo para comer.	There is time to eat.
Hay un asiento disponible.	There is an available seat.
Hay un baño atrás.	There is a bathroom in the back.

Statement plural: There are _____.

Hay boletos a Mérida.	There are tickets to Merida.
Hay mucha gente en la fila.	There are a lot of people in line.
Hay burritos en venta.	There are burritos for sale.
Hay niños en el tren.	There are children in the train.

Question singular: Is there _____.

¿Hay lugar para comer?	Is there a place to eat?
¿Hay una lámpara para leer?	Is there a lamp for reading?
¿Hay espacio para la maleta?	Is there space for the suitcase?
¿Hay música abordo?	Is there music on board?
¿Hay WIFI en el camión?	Is there WIFI on the bus?

Question plural: Are there _____.

¿Hay turistas en el tren?	Are there tourists on the train?
¿Hay almohadas en el tren?	Are there pillows on the train?
¿ Hay refrescos?	Are there refreshments?
¿Hay extranjeros abordo?	Are there foreigners on board?
¿Hay muchos escalones?	Are there many steps?

If you want to say "no there is not," or "no, there are not," it's simple! Just place the word NO before the sentence and it is negated!

E.g.	*¿Hay costo para entrar?*	Is there a cost to enter?
	¿Cobran la entrada?	Is there a charge to get in?

You can answer questions with *"Hay"*?
Affirmative:	*Sí, si ha*	Yes, there is.
Negative:	*No, no hay*	No, there isn't.

Growing Your Sandwich Spanish

Word Wheel with Key Pivot Practice

Pivot 1: Hay (pronounced 'eye')_____. = There is/are_____.

"Hay" is an extremely high-frequency word that can be used in just about any situation! While only a three-letter word, it can immediately improve your Spanish! This short word can be used for four different functions: Singular and plural statements, and questions!

Your turn! Practice using the center pivot to create numerous sentences in Spanish! Be creative by using everything you have learned in this lesson and beyond!

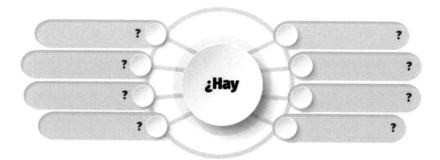

Cultural Cue: The idea of personal space differs from country to country. Most of the world is different from western cultures. While traveling abroad, personal space can be smaller than one is used to. So, to enjoy your travel, keep in mind that you may not have as much space on a bus or train as you are used to, but in time, you can get used to it and begin to feel comfortable. Give yourself time to adjust.

Pivot 2: ¿Cuánto cuesta___? = How much does____cost?

¿Cuánto cuesta? is used anywhere you are looking for a price, but you can also use the short form, *"cuánto"* which is "how much" as we do in English. We say, "how much does this cost," or if we are indicating what it is, simply, "how much." It is how we naturally speak!

Your turn! Practice using the center pivot to create numerous sentences in Spanish! Be creative by using everything you have learned in this lesson and beyond!

> **Pronunciation Tip:** Be true to the vowels when pronouncing these words. A vowel is equal to a syllable, which is a beat, So, you cannot cheat the word, or shorten the vowel. Remember that 'E' is long 'A' in English as in "rate". So, be sure you can hear it.

Pivot 3: Me gustaría pagar___. = I would like to pay (for)__.

"Me gustaría" is the **polite alternative** to *"quiero"*. It is used to make a request that you are not sure will be fulfilled. It is the polite form when asking for something, or when expressing a desire to do something. In this case it is to pay for a good or service.

Your turn! Practice using the center pivot to create numerous sentences in Spanish! Be creative by using everything you have learned in this lesson and beyond!

> **Pronunciation Tip:** Remember! Go back to the five pure vowels and the 12 exceptions so that your pronunciation will be clear and native-like! You will feel more confident to speak and improve your skills if you can get close to those sounds!

Pivot 4: ¿Me da __ por favor? = Can you give me __please?

"Me da" means give me, as in a request. You are asking, "can you give this to me?" It is always followed by a concrete or abstract thing, **but not an action.**

Your turn! Practice using the center pivot to create numerous sentences in Spanish! Be creative by using everything you have learned in this lesson and beyond!

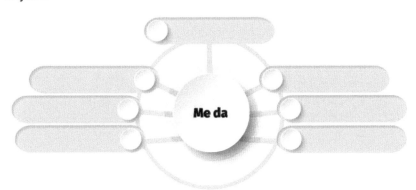

Pronunciation Tip: The letter 'D' is not hard as in English but is always pronounced as soft 'TH'. Be sure to produce it with your tongue softly between your teeth. This is probably one of the best tips to assure native-like Spanish when you speak. It will sound like "may tha".

Pivot 5: ¿A qué hora sale__? = At what time does__leave?

This can be used to ask about any **public transportation.** You can substitute *"sale"* with *"regresa"*, or returns, as the center pivot, and you can use the same words in the wheel to make more sentences.

E.g.   *¿A qué hora regresa el tour?*
         What time does the tour return/end?
         You can use it for *el camión, el tren*, etc.

Your turn! Practice using the center pivot to create numerous sentences in Spanish! Be creative by using everything you have learned in this lesson and beyond!

Pronunciation Tip: The 'H' in Spanish is one of the exceptions. It is always silent in "hospital" and "honor," for example. In "alcohol" the each 'O' become one, sounding like alcol. The exception to this is when 'H' is next to the letter 'C', as in *"hecho"*. Together they are pronounced as 'CH', just like in English.

Expanding your Spanish:
More Key Pivot Practice

Use the *Spanish Sandwich* method (bread-meat-bread), the dressings, the key pivots, the sides, and all you know about the sounds to create your own sandwich. Also, use cognates, or words that come from the same origin, to recall words you already know. Bring these all together and make your own unique Spanish sandwiches!

¡Adelante!   *Go ahead!*

Bread:

Meat:

Bread:

Bread:

Meat:

Bread:

Bread:

Meat:

Bread:

Bread:

Meat:

Bread:

Cultural Cue: Remember, language IS social, and **practice makes permanent**! The better you feel, the more confident you are and the more you will use it! And the cycle continues.

Common Travel Expressions

Now you can enhance your *Sandwich Spanish* by using these phrases to communicate in any travel setting. Use what you know about the vowels and consonants to sound like a native! Practice them whenever you can!

Me gustaría un viaje redondo.	I would like a round trip ticket.
Me gustaría un viaje sencillo.	I would like a one way.
Vamos de viaje.	Let's go/we are going on a trip.
Vamos de vacaciones.	Let's go/we are going on vacation.
Vamos a la luna de miel.	Let's go/we are going on a honeymoon.
¡Qué viaje tan largo!	What a long trip!
¿Ya llegamos?	Are we there yet?
¿Dónde está la parada del taxi?	Where is the taxi stand?
No entiendo mucho español.	I don't understand much Spanish.
¿Hablas inglés?	Do you speak English?

Cultural Cue: When you ask someone for the time, you use *"¿me da la hora?"* or *"¿me da su hora?"* This is the polite way to say, "What time is it?" You are politely asking them, "Can you give me your hour?"

Wrap it up &
Take it To Go!

What I Can Politely Do In Native-Like Spanish:

- Ask about departures.

- Inquire about prices and buy tickets.

- Find the bathroom.

- Ask if there are food or services on the train or plane.

- Get information about my luggage.

- Find out when I will leave and arrive.

- Can pronounce all five pure vowels in Spanish.

- What else can you do?

I Am Culturally Skilled To: Interact with others respectfully and confidently while traveling by bus or train, and to feel comfortable traveling to my destination.

¡Buen viaje!   Have a great trip!

Topic Bundle 3

Hotel and Resort

My story: hotels are the place to make friends

We eventually moved to Toluca and were staying at the Motel Del Rey until our home was ready. As I was having breakfast there my daughter Samira, who was almost two, managed to get locked in the bathroom with David, the son of our now-dear friends Vira and Tony from Portugal.

We both panicked and informed the staff that our children were locked in the bathroom. Our Spanish was skimpy, so Vira told them in Portuguese! I guess it worked as they finally got them out. Both kids were playing and laughing as children do when we finally got the door unlocked. The moms, well, we were frazzled! This incident led to a lot of fun in Toluca and a lifelong friendship!

Sandwich Spanish Ingredients

Hotel and Resort Stays

In this chapter, we are using *Sandwich Spanish* to function in a hotel or resort. You will enjoy the wonderful hospitality of the region, while getting absolutely spoiled. What else is more pleasurable and satisfying than learning to speak Spanish to have a comfortable vacation where others can understand you and answer to your every whim! Let's taste a piece of your sandwich.

The Bread: Step 1: Greeting

Politely get attention. Always begin with: **Buenos días, buenas tardes, or buenas noches.** *Notice that we only use "buenos" in the morning!*

Disculpa, discúlpame.	Excuse me.
Perdón, perdonáme. ¿Que dijo?	Excuse me. What did you say?
Señor.	Sir, or Mr.
Señora.	Married woman.
Señorita.	Single woman, or if uncertain.

The Meat: Step 2: Communicate Purpose

Things you would like to ask at a hotel or resort.

Tenemos reservación para dos.	We have a reservation for two.
Prefiero una cama king, por favor.	I prefer a king size bed, please.
¿En qué piso está el gimnasio?	Which floor is the gym on?
¿El cuarto tiene minibar?	Does the room have a minibar?
¿Es posible quedar más días?	Is it possible to stay longer?
¿Cobran el uso de la alberca?	Do you charge to use the pool?
¿Aquí es todo incluído?	Is this place all-inclusive?
¿Podemos dejar las maletas aquí?	Can we leave our suitcases here?
¿Nos puede llamar un taxi?	Can you call us a taxi?
¿Hay un conserje aquí (En el hotel)?	Is there a concierge here?
¿Tienen servicio al cuarto?	Do you have room service?
¿A qué hora es la salida?	What time is check out?

The Bread: Step 3: Appreciate And Depart

Things you would ask or say after getting help with your trip.

Gracias por su ayuda.	Thank you for your help.
Gracias, muy amable.	Thank you. It's very kind of you.
Está bien, gracias.	It's fine, thank you.
¡Nos encantó! ¡Me encantó!	We loved it.

Sandwich Spanish Condiments

Spice up your Sandwich with these 'Condiments'!

Cuarto/habitación	Room
Recepción	Reception/front desk
Elevador	Elevator
Cama matrimonial, Queen, King	Full, queen, king-size bed
Piso	Floor
Restaurante	Restaurant
Actividades	Activities
Cobros extras	Extra charges
Cobrar aparte (extra)	Additional charges
Todo incluído	All-inclusive
El gerente	The manager
Ruido	Noise
Limpiar	To clean
Servicio de tintorería	Dry cleaning service
Servicio de lavandaría	Laundry service
La recamarera	The room attendant
La televisión	The television
Sirve, no sirve	It works/it doesn't work
El aire	Air conditioning
Pedir	To ask/order something
Servicio a la habitación	Room service
Almohada	Pillow
Sábanas	Sheets
Apartar	To reserve

Variations For Your Word Wheel

"Tienen" is a very valuable word to know, as it is used similar to *"hay"*. You can ask if a store has something while shopping using either one, and they can both be used to make a statement or ask a question.

¿Tienen té negro?	Do you have (sell, carry) black tea?
¿Hay té negro?	Do you have (sell, carry) black tea?

"Tienen" and "Hay" can be used for *the* **same intention** as in English.

Statements:	**You have/there are_____ .**
Tienen mucha genteen el hotel hoy.	You have a lot of people in the hotel today.
Hay mucha gente en el hotel hoy.	There are a lot of people in the hotel today.

Questions:	**Do you have/are there_____ .**
¿Tienen mucha gente hoy?	Do you have a lot of people today?
¿Hay mucha gente hoy?	Are there a lot of people today?

Es = "It is" at the beginning and "is" in the middle of sentences

"Es" is always equal to "it is" for a statement and "is it" for a question when it is at the beginning of a sentence. When it is somewhere in the middle, it is just "is". This is wonderful because it is one of the highest frequency words in Spanish which means it will serve you often in a variety of conversations!

Es mi hermana	It's my sister (on the phone, in a picture)
Ella es mi hermana	She is my sister
Es mi marido	It's my husband (at the door)
Él es mi marido	He is my husband

"Es posible" is followed by an action word or a time word

¿Es posible nadar en la alberca?	Is it possible to swim in the pool?
¿Es posible hoy?	Is it possible today?

Growing Your Sandwich Spanish

Word Wheel with Key Pivot Practice

Pivot 1: Prefiero_____. = I prefer_____.

"Prefiero" is a commonly used word, especially when offering your preference in a variety of situations. You can add a thing or an action to it to complete your expression. **It is a high-frequency word** that you will find yourself using often when you are offered a choice.

Your turn! Practice using the center pivot to create numerous sentences in Spanish! Be creative by using everything you have learned in this lesson and beyond!

> **Cultural Cue:** It is very important to remember your *Sandwich Spanish* when interacting with native speakers. You will show respect for their culture. If you care to make a good impression of your home culture, be a 'good guest'. You do not want to be labeled *"mal educado/educada"* or rude!

Pivot 2: Tienen_____? = You have/do you have_____?

You know that *"tienen"* is a **versatile word** that can make statements and questions, can be used to go shopping, or to get any information about a specific item.

Your turn! Practice using the center pivot to create numerous sentences in Spanish! Be creative by using everything you have learned in this lesson and beyond!

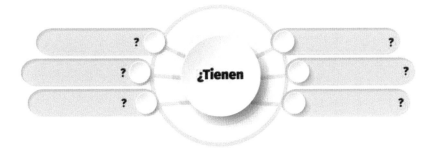

Pronunciation Tip: Remember that you only have to master five vowels sounds that are pure and never change! It is also important to take a pause and go back to the introduction about the vowels. They are not long, as in English, but shorter and only have one movement of the mouth! If your mouth is moving to make two sounds, try to stop it after one. It will sound shorter than English vowels.

Pivot 3: ¿Cobran_____? = Do you charge (for)_____?

When we want to know if there is an extra charge for something, or we simply want to know the conditions of the payment for a service or product, we can use "cobran". **It is a broad pivot** that can be followed by a variety of words that tell us when, how, and for what we are paying.

Your turn! Practice using the center pivot to create numerous sentences in Spanish! Be creative by using everything you have learned in this lesson and beyond!

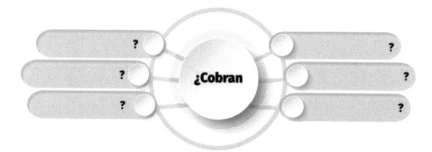

Pronunciation Tip: Remember! Go back to the five pure vowels and the 12 consonant exceptions so that your pronunciation will be clear and native-like! You will feel more confident to speak and improve your skills if you can get close to those sounds! Try to bring out the 'R' by separating it from the 'B'. This will allow you to form the "rolled r" sound. With practice it will get easier. Don't let it get lost in the word!

Pivot 4: ¿Podemos_____? = We can/can we_____?

"Podemos" means "we can" or "can we"? It can only be followed by **any action word**. You can use it to offer help, ask if you are able to do something, or get permission to do something.

Your turn! Practice using the center pivot to create numerous sentences in Spanish! Be creative by using everything you have learned in this lesson and beyond!

> **Pronunciation Tip:** In the introduction, you learned that Spanish is an CVC (Consonant-Vowel-Consonant) language. When you pronounce "podemos", give it time and clearly say each syllable. A vowel is a syllable, so we cannot omit them or give them less value and still be understood. Begin slowly to be sure that you aren't inserting "short vowels" that do not exist in Spanish. This is what will bring you closer to a native accent. Remember the 'D' in Spanish is a soft 'TH'.

Pivot 5: ¿Es posible_____? = Is it possible_____?

This pivot is only used alongside an action word. You can use it, add one word, and have a complete sentence! You can make a question by simply **adjusting your intonation.**

Your turn! Practice using the center pivot to create numerous sentences in Spanish! Be creative by using everything you have learned in this lesson and beyond!

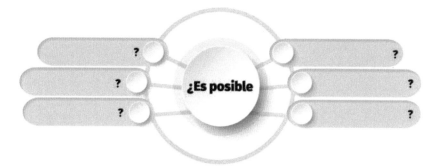

Pronunciation Tip: The 'E' in *"Es"* is pronounced like "ace" in a deck of cards, so be sure it is clear. The 'E' at the end of "possible" is pronounced as 'A' as in "late". With practice, you will automatically use these and it will greatly improve your accent.

Expanding your Spanish:
More Key Pivot Practice

Use the *Spanish Sandwich* method (bread-meat-bread), the dressings, the key pivots, the sides, and all you know about the sounds to create your own sandwich. Also, use cognates, or words that come from the same origin, to recall words you already know. Bring these all together and make your own unique Spanish sandwiches!

¡Adelante!   *Go ahead!*

Bread:

Meat:

Bread:

Bread:

Meat:

Bread:

Bread:

Meat:

Bread:

Bread:

Meat:

Bread:

Cultural Cue: When you are a guest or traveler, it is important to follow cultural norms for behavior. Loud or boisterous behavior is not acceptable, nor is excessive drinking, impatient remarks, or a demanding tone. Your *Sandwich Spanish* will help you stay within that norm by using greetings and appreciation when you communicate at a hotel or resort. A gentle demeanor and a smile will also add to making any interaction in Spanish a pleasant and enjoyable one.

Common Hotel And Resort Expressions

Now you can enhance your *Sandwich Spanish* by using these phrases to communicate in any hotel or resort setting. Use what you know about the vowels and consonants to sound like a native! Practice them whenever you can!

Me gustaría mandar a lavar la ropa.	I'd like to send my clothes to wash.
¿Me da otra llave?	Can you give me another room key?
Necesito la caja de seguridad	I need the safety deposit box.
¿Nos presta una cuna?	Can you loan us a crib?
¿Tiene servicio de niñeras?	Do you have babysitting services?
¿Hay un doctor en el hotel (resort)?	Is there a doctor in the hotel?
¿Podemos cambiar de cuarto?	May we change rooms?
Me gustaría dejar un mensaje.	I would like to leave a message.
¿Me presta una secadora?	Can you loan me a hair dryer?
¿Me da un cepillo de dientes?	Can you give me a toothbrush?
¿Hay transporte al restaurant?	Is there a shuttle to the restaurant?
¿Es posible quedar otra noche?	Is it possible to stay another night?

Cultural Cue: Most Latin American countries are generally conservative in behavior, so loud and boisterous conduct is rarely accepted. As a guest, it is important to avoid confrontation and to stay calm, especially if things are taking longer than you might expect. Remember, for them, time is flexible, relaxed, and circular, and is therefore unlimited.

Communication styles are subtle and not so "in your face". Try to go with the flow and relax. Things usually get done and get done well! Remember, you are a guest in their country, so always aim to be a gracious one!

Wrap it up & Take it To Go!

What I Can Politely Do In Native-Like Spanish:

- Check into a hotel or resort.

- Express my preferences.

- Ask about the details of my room.

- Ask about the hotel or resort services.

- Talk about possibilities.

- Find out what we are able to do at the hotel or resort.

- Pronounce all five vowels in Spanish.

- What else can you do?

I Am Culturally Skilled To: Interact with others respectfully and confidently at a hotel or resort, and I feel comfortable getting my needs met there.

¡Bienvenidos!   Welcome!

Topic Bundle 4

Entertainment and Fun

My story: language is social, right?

One of the thrills of living just outside of the cosmopolitan, multicultural capital of Mexico City was the amazing entertainment! Like New York City, there were concerts, plays, amusement parks, theatres, museums, and world class restaurants! The best live shows I saw were Evita and Jesus Christ Superstar! What spectacular talent! They also put my novice Spanish to the test! I am sure my husband and in-laws were tired of me asking "What did they say." Wow, what a great way to learn Spanish!

I then added the "novelas' to my Spanish learning and really began to understand and mimic more. After traveling to many of the 32 states in Mexico and enjoying Mexican cities, it turns out that most offer a plethora of activities for everyone's taste! Bienvenidos a México - A window of opportunity to learn and understand a diverse, ancient, yet modern culture!

Sandwich Spanish Ingredients

Finding entertainment and fun

In this chapter, we are using *Sandwich Spanish* to enjoy entertainment and fun! Typically, each city and town offers a variety of activities for wonderful entertainment including movies, live theatre, country and health clubs, water sports, etc. What else is more pleasurable and satisfying than learning to speak Spanish so that you can enjoy life? Let's taste a piece of your sandwich

The Bread - Step 1: Greeting

Politely get attention. Always begin with: **Buenos días, buenas tardes, or buenas noches**. *Notice that we only use "buenos" in the morning!*

Disculpa, discúlpame.	Excuse me.
Perdón, perdóname. ¿Qué dijo?	Excuse me. What did you say?
Señor.	Sir, or Mr.
Señora.	Married woman
Señorita.	Single woman, or if uncertain.

The Meat - Step 2: Communicate Purpose

Things you would ask if you are wanting to relax or have fun.

Vamos al cine.	Let's go to the movies.
¿Hay música en vivo en el Lido?	Is there live music at the Lido?
¿Dónde hay lugar para bailar?	Where is there a place to dance?
¿Sabes de una buena hora feliz?	Do you know of a good happy hour?
¿Hay excursiones a otras partes?	Are there excursions to other places?
¿Quién tiene los boletos?	Who has the tickets?
¿Dónde hay playas bonitas?	Where are there beautiful beaches?
¿Los eventos están en Facebook?	Are the events on Facebook?
¿Hay cines aquí?	Are there movie theatres here?
¿Dónde es posible pescar?	Where is it possible to fish?
¿Dónde hay un campo de golf?	Where is there a golf course?

¿Cuánto cobran para jugar golf?	How much do they charge to play golf?
¿Qué incluye?	What is included?
Dónde está el teatro de la ciudad?	Where is the city theatre?
Quién va a tocar?	Who is playing?

The Bread - Step 3: Appreciate And Depart

Things you would ask or say after getting help with your trip.

Gracias por su ayuda.	Thank you for your help.
Gracias, muy amable.	Thank you. It's very kind of you.
Gracias por la información.	Thank you for the information.
¡Nos vemos en el cine!	See you at the movies!

> **Remember:** You don't need to translate word for word: just accept the phrases and their meaning. Learn to use them in conversation without the need to know each word. Accept the language and culture the way it is!

Sandwich Spanish Condiments

Spice up your Sandwich with these 'Condiments'!

Apartar boletos	To reserve tickets
Reservar un lugar	To book a place
Tomar un tour	To take a tour
Asistir a una obra	To attend a play
Asistir un concierto/show	To attend a concert/show
Comprar boletos	To buy tickets
Jugar golf, tenis, etc.	To play golf, tennis, etc.
Pedir un lugar	To request a place
Tomar un coctail	To drink a cocktail
Bucear y esnorkel	To scuba dive and snorkel
Rentar una lancha	To rent a boat

Ver las ruinas	To see the ruins
Conocer los cenotes	To visit the underground waters
Tomar un viaje de dia	To take a day trip
Disfrutar de los museos	To enjoy the museums
Invitar a mis amigos	To invite my friends
Tener una boda	To have a wedding
Actividades acuáticos	Water activities
Actividades sociales	Social activities
Actividades de la comunidad	Community activities
Actividades educativos	Educational activities

> **Note:** You can see many action words in this list, which are used exactly the way you see them! You can use them in your word wheels with the pivots to make real sentences. In the previous bundles you can see *"me gustaría"*. Just add any of these action words:

Me gustaría conocer a los cenotes	I would like to visit the cenotes
Me gustaría invitar a mis amigos	I would like to invite my friends
Me gustaría asistir al juego de fútbol	I would like to attend the football game

Variations For Your Word Wheel

In this bundle, you can see several action words that are used just the way they are! You do not have to change them! It does not matter how they end, they all have the same job! You just want to have fun and enjoy yourself, so keep it simple!

Now you can begin to use what you have learned to this point. You know "tiene" and "hay" and can use them to ask for information. So, build your conversation with your Spanish Sandwiches. Here are two examples:

1. Greeting/attention getter:

You: *Buenos días señor. Disculpa*

Purpose:

You:	*¿Hay boletos para el tour a las ruinas (a Chichen Itza)?*
Agent:	*Sí, si hay.*
You:	*Bueno (ok). Me gustaría comprar dos boletos para las ruinas de Tulum.*
Agent:	*Esta bien (ok). Son dos cientos pesos.*

Appreciate and depart:

You:	*Muchas gracias. Muy amable.*
Agent:	*De nada. Buen viaje.*

2. Greeting/attention getter:

You: Buen día señorita. Discúlpame.

Purpose:

You:	*¿Hay música en vivo hoy?*
Senorita:	*Sí, si hay a las ocho.*
You:	*Bueno. Me gustaría apartar una mesa, por favor.*
Senorita:	*Muy bien. Una mesa para las ocho. ¿Para cuántas personas?*
You:	*Para cuatro.*
Senorita:	*Muy bien. Cuatro personas para las ocho.*

Appreciate and depart:

You: *Muchísimas gracias.*

Senorita: *Nos vemos a las ocho. Que le vaya bien.*

You: *Gracias, adios.*

> **Note:** Remember that you do not have to go any further to change the words. Everything is here for you. Just make it fit your needs and speak Spanish!

Vamos a: making suggestions for an activity, or to go somewhere.

Vamos a = Let's. We use this in English when we want to make a suggestion to those we are with. When we use *"vamos a"*, we must use an action word or a place.

Action Word:

Vamos a nadar en el Caribe	Let's swim in the Caribbean

A Place or Destination:

Vamos al mar	Let's go to the shore
Vamos a Mérida	Let's to to Merida
Vamos a la casa de mi amiga	Let's go to my friend's house

When we use "vamos a", we look at the word that follows: is it a girl or a boy?

"El mar" is a male word. So, we combine "a" and "el" to get "AL":
E.g.   *Vamos al mar.* (not "vamos a el mar")

"La fiesta" is a female word, so there's no need to combine:
E.g.   *Vamos a la fiesta.*

Asking for information

"Quién" always means "who" when we want to ask a question:

¿Quién es tu esposa?	Who is your wife?
Kathy es mi esposa	Kathy is my wife

"Dónde" always means "where" in any conversation:

¿Dónde hay un hospital?	Where is there a hospital?
Hay en el centro	There is one downtown

"Qué" usually means "what". It can also mean that, which, who, etc. depending on the usage and context. See: http://www.spanishdict.com/translate/que

Que	What?
¿Qué incluye en el precio?	What is included in the price?
Incluye comida y un trago	It includes lunch and one alcoholic drink
Que	That
¿Sábes que no hay agua?	Did you know that there is no water?

Growing Your Sandwich Spanish

Word Wheel with Key Pivot Practice

Pivot 1: Vamos a_____. = Let's_____.

Using *"vamos a"* is the best way to suggest a place or activity! Remember that the "a" becomes "al" before a male word, but before a female word, it stays the same. The 'V' at the beginning, sounds like a 'B' vibrating between your lips! This sound will allow you to speak like a native Spanish speaker!

Your turn! Practice using the center pivot to create numerous sentences in Spanish! Be creative by using everything you have learned in this lesson and beyond

Cultural Cue: In most Latin cultures, the one who invites usually means the one who pays for the check. Be sure to be clear if you are inviting someone as "your treat", or *"cada quien paga"* (each one pays). This will keep things clear and conflict free. If you plan to pay you say, *"te invito"* (I am inviting you). As the expression goes, *"cuentas claras, amistades largas"*, or "clear accounts make for long friendships".

Pivot 2: ¿Donde hay__? = Where is (are)/where can I find __?

"Dónde hay" is used to ask where you can find a **specific place, service, or thing**. It comes in handy when shopping, asking for directions, or finding someone who can provide a specific service in your home. It can also mean "where can I find _____?"

Your turn! Practice using the center pivot to create numerous sentences in Spanish! Be creative by using everything you have learned in this lesson and beyond!

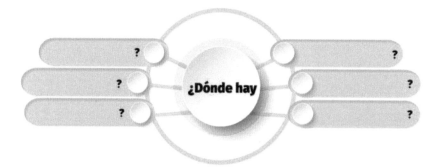

> **Pronunciation Tip:** *"Dónde"* has two D's which are pronounced as such. The first one is with the tongue slightly between the teeth, and the second one with the tongue between the teeth. Neither one is a hard 'D' as in English! Get it right, and you will sound like a native speaker! Don't be afraid to bite your tongue!

Pivot 3: ¿Incluye _____? = Does it include _____?

"Incluye _____?: is used to ask if a **specific item or service** is included in the base price you are being charged. It can be used for paying for meals, tours, or any services you purchase.

Your turn! Practice using the center pivot to create numerous sentences in Spanish! Be creative by using everything you have learned in this lesson and beyond!

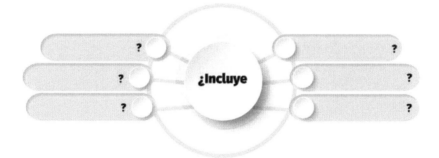

Pronunciation Tip: The 'I' in Spanish is the same as the long 'E' as in "meet". Be careful not to say the English "in". This is important as it is noticable when you speak if you are trying to sound native-like.

Pivot 4: ¿Quien va a _____? = Who is going to _____?

"Quién va a" is used to ask who is going to do something, or who is going to a specific place. It is useful for making plans or finding out who is responsible for an action. You can add a place, an event, or an action word to complete the sentence.

Your turn! Practice using the center pivot to create numerous sentences in Spanish! Be creative by using everything you have learned in this lesson and beyond!

Pronunciation Tip: When a word ends in a vowel and the next word begins in the same vowel, the two seem to merge into one sound and one syllable. "Va a" become only "va". When a male word follows "va a", we must say *"va al cine"*, since "a" is combined with the *"el"* of cine (two beats). For a female word that follows, use *"va a la playa"* (three beats). E.g. *¿Quién va a la fiesta? ¿Quién va al cine?*

Pivot 5: ¿Cuanto cobran___? = How much do they charge___?

"Cuanto cobran" is used to ask a price for a good or service. It means "how much do you (they) charge for", or "how much does the place of business charge". **It can be used alone.**

Your turn! Practice using the center pivot to create numerous sentences in Spanish! Be creative by using everything you have learned in this lesson and beyond!

> **Pronunciation Tip:** Since we know Spanish is a CVC language, we can also use this notion to improve pronunciation. When we use "cuanto cobran", it is important to avoid a breath before "cobran". The two words can be pronounced almost as one word. Just count four beats

Expanding your Spanish:
More Key Pivot Practice

Use the *Spanish Sandwich* method (bread-meat-bread), the dressings, the key pivots, the sides, and all you know about the sounds to create your own sandwich. Also, use cognates, or words that come from the same origin, to recall words you already know. Bring these all together and make your own unique Spanish sandwiches!

¡Adelante! *Go ahead!*

Bread:

Meat:

Bread:

Bread:

Meat:

Bread:

Bread:

Meat:

Bread:

Bread:

Meat:

Bread:

Cultural Cue: As gracious guests it is always important to remember to respect the host culture. This means that while visiting historical sites, ruins, museums, etc., we must do so with honor and reverence. Many sites are UNESCO World Heritage sites and showcase the history and legacies which are the pride of the locals. Be sure to research the sites before you go, so that you can appreciate their beauty and significance to the world. Show respect and interest while visiting, and remember you are also representing your own country and culture, so always be at your best.

Common Recreation And Fun Expressions

Now you can enhance your *Sandwich Spanish* by using these phrases to communicate in any recreational and fun entertainment venue or situation. Use what you know about the vowels and consonants to sound like a native! Practice them whenever you can!

Vamos a pasear.	Let's check things out.
Vamos a dar la vuelta.	Let's go for a walk/ride.
¡Qué divertido!	How fun!
¿Te gustó?	Did you like it?
¿Cómo te fue?	How was it?
¡Se acabó!	It is over/it finished.
¿Cómo jugaste?	How did you play/how was the game?
¡Qué bonito lugar!	What a beautiful place!
¡Tengo ganas de pizza!	I feel like eating pizza!
¡Qué grande hotel!	What a huge hotel!
¡Qué calor aquí!	It's so hot here!
¡Me gustó mucho!	I liked it a lot!
¿Incluye café con el precio?	Is the coffee included in the price?
¡Disfruto mucho a México!	I really enjoy Mexico!
¡Vámonos!	Let's go/let's get out of here!

Cultural Cue: A traveler heading to Latin America can find the best recommendations and ideas for fun and entertainment online. Specifically, Meetups, Facebook groups and other popular social media platforms are great ways to find ideas and reviews. Contacting businesses for reservations and information is best done using WhatsApp, which is free to use and is commonly the main way to communicate with the locals. Websites such as Tripadvisor and Yelp are also helpful when planning for a fun time!

Wrap it up & Take it To Go!

What I Can Politely Do In Native-Like Spanish:

- Suggest activities and places to go.

- Find out where specific places are located.

- Ask questions using who, where, and what.

- Ask if anyone knows a specific person, place, or event.

- Ask about who is going to perform.

- Use common expressions about entertainment events.

- What else can you do?

I am culturally skilled to: Interact with others respectfully and confidently while seeking relaxing and fun activities, and using Spanish to get my needs met.

¡Que te diviertas!   *Have a good time!*

Topic Bundle 5
Socializing with Neighbors

My story: being neighborly – a new meaning in Spanish

As a young couple, we were able to buy our first home in Santiago Miltepec, on the outskirts of Toluca proper. It was a kind of row home, with lovely red tile floors which later served as our expats party dance floor!

When we arrived, I met a sweet neighbor who was friendly and kind to us. She was a character for sure as everyday she greeted us with honey and avocado on her face! It seemed she never washed it off and her two sons and husband seemed to take it as her natural look! With them, I was obliged to practice my Spanish since none of them spoke English! What a great opportunity! I felt great improvement as I was immersed in Spanish with this amazing family!

And, I even got a few natural "beauty tips" from our neighbor along the way!

Sandwich Spanish Ingredients

Socializing with the neighbors

In this chapter, we are using *Sandwich Spanish* to interact and converse with the neighbors. Typically, neighbors are friendly and might know a bit of English, but what a surprise if you can break the ice in Spanish! What is more pleasurable than learning to speak Spanish so that you can get to know native speakers and build friendships? Let's taste a piece of your sandwich.

The Bread: Step 1: Greeting

Politely get attention. Always begin with: **Buenos días, buenas tardes, or buenas noches.** *Notice that we only use "buenos" in the morning!*

¿Buenos días, qué tal?	Good day, how are things?
¿Hola, qué onda, cómo estás?	Hi, what's up, how are things?
¿Buen día, cómo le va?	Good day, how is it going?
¿Hola Beto, qué haces?	Hi Beto, what are you up to?

The Meat Step 2: Communicate Purpose

Things you would ask to make small talk and socialize for the first time.

Soy Kathy.	I am Kathy.
¿De dónde eres?	Where are you from?
Soy de Canadá.	I am from Canada.
¿Qué haces?	What do you do?
¿Qué hacías?	What did you do (before retiring)?
¿Estás jubilado/a?	Are you retired?
Estoy jubilado/a.	I am retired.
¿Eres casado ó soltero?	Are you married or single?
¿Tienes hijos?	Do you have children?
¿Tienes nietos?	Do you have grandchildren?
¿Cuánto tiempo tienes aquí?	How long have you been here?
Mi esposa es Kathy.	My wife is Kathy.

Tengo cuatro años aquí	I have been here four years.
¿Eres residente?	Are you a resident?
Sí, soy residente.	Yes, I am a resident.
Mucho gusto.	Nice to meet you.
Igualmente.	Same here.

The Bread: Step 3: Appreciate And Depart

Bueno, gusto en saludarte.	Ok, nice talking with you.
Igualmente, fue un placer.	Same here, it was a pleasure meeting you.
Vamos a estar en contacto.	Let's stay in touch.
Adios. Que le vaya bien..	Goodbye. Hope all goes well for you.

Sandwich Spanish Condiments

Spice up your Sandwich with these 'Condiments'!

Los Estados Unidos	The United States
Nietos	Grandchildren (male/both genders)
Nietas	Granddaughters
Hijos	Children (male/both)
Hijas	Daughters
Esposo/a	Husband/wife
Soy plomero	I am a plumber
Soy electricista	I am an electrician.
Soy gerente de ventas	I am a sales manager
Fui trailero	I was a truck driver
Fui abogado	I was a lawyer
Suegro/a	Father in law/mother in law
Yerno	Son in law
Nuera	Daughter in law
Abuelo/a	Grandfather/grandmother
Primo/a	Cousin
Casado	Married
Soltero	Single
Divorciado/a	Divorced
Viudo/a	Widowed
Mi	My
Tú	Your
Mío	Mine
Tuyo	Yours

Yo Y Tú/Me And You

These are the only two forms that you need to know to begin to make small talk and get to know someone. Each word has its partner, so you can always tell what to answer by listening to the question carefully. **The answer is hiding in the question!**

You	I
¿De dónde eres?	**Soy de Houston, Texas.**
Where are you from?	I am from Houston, Texas.
¿Tienes hijos?	**Sí, tengo tres hijos.**
Do you have children?	Yes, I have three children.
¿Tienes nietos?	**No, no tengo nietos todavía.**
Do you have grandchildren?	No, I don't have any yet.
¿Eres casado?	**Sí, soy casado. Mi esposa es Kathy**
Are you married?	Yes, I am married. My wife is Kathy.
¿Estás jubilado?	**Sí, estoy jubilado.**
Are you retired?	Yes, I am retired.

Soy and Eres

"Soy" is used to talk about yourself when things most likely will not change. *"Eres"* is used for the person you are talking to when things most likely will not change.

Questions with "tienes" always use "tengo" to answer

¿Cuánto tiempo	**tienes**	**aquí?**
How long	have you been	here?
Tengo	**seis meses**	
I have been here	six months.	

Note: Sometimes you hear *"¿cuánto tienes aquí?"* The answer is still *"tengo seis meses."*

¿Cuánto tiempo	**tienes trabajando**	**en Ford?**
How long	have you worked	at Ford?
Tengo trabajando	**en Ford**	**diez años.**
I have worked	at Ford	for ten years.

Growing Your Sandwich Spanish

Word Wheel with Key Pivot Practice

Pivot 1: Soy_____. = I am_____.

"Soy" is used very often in a variety of topics when you want to describe yourself. It is used for things that **are not likely to change**. It can sometimes be confused with *"estoy"* which is also "I am", but only when you are describing things that **can change at any time**. This change depends greatly on the situation.

Your turn! Practice using the center pivot to create numerous sentences in Spanish! Be creative by using everything you have learned in this lesson and beyond!

> **Cultural Cue:** In Latin cultures you will find that most people are very warm and friendly. They enjoy making conversation especially with neighbors. Whether you know them or not, they will always greet you regardless of the time of day and will always expect a response. Neighbors will usually help one another when necessary. Use this opportunity to practice as much as you can. You may make a friend in the process!

Pivot 2: ¿Eres_____? = You are _____?

"Eres" is used when you talk to one person directly in conversation. It is used to **make a statement or a question.** *"¿Eres mi amigo?"* (Are you my friend?) is the same as *"Eres my amigo".* (You are my friend.)

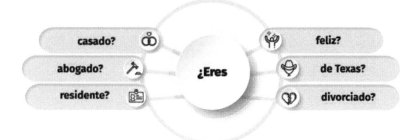

Your turn! Practice using the center pivot to create numerous sentences in Spanish! Be creative by using everything you have learned in this lesson and beyond!

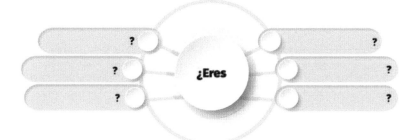

Pronunciation Tip: The sound of 'E' is always a long as in "ate". Be sure that both sounds are the same and have the same duration! Say the vowels first, then fill in the consonants! It will work to give you a native-like accent.

Pivot 3: ¿Sábes de____? = Do you know of any / anyone who ____

When you have a specific need for any service, you can use this to get **recommendations** from others. *"¿Sábes de_____?"* is great if you are new to an area and want to get the best price and quality service.

Your turn! Practice using the center pivot to create numerous sentences in Spanish! Be creative by using everything you have learned in this lesson and beyond!

Pronunciation Tip: You know that the 'B' in Spanish is between the 'V' and 'B; rather than a hard sound as in English. Also, remember that the 'D' is 'DE', is like a soft 'TH'. These two sounds are easily the two that can best give you a native accent, or at least get you close. You will begin to sound more and more like a native speaker!

Pivot 4: ¿Tienes____? = Do you have ___?

"¿Tienes _____?" can be used in a **variety of situations** and is especially useful in getting to know someone. You can ask someone about things, or relationships. You can also use it when shopping, or looking for something specific.

Your turn! Practice using the center pivot to create numerous sentences in Spanish! Be creative by using everything you have learned in this lesson and beyond!

Pronunciation Tip: You can really impact your accent in Spanish by making the 'T' sound softer than the 'T' in English. In Spanish, there is no puff of air after the sound so you can practice it by holding your hand to your mouth. If you feel air, you know you need to adjust it so that it is softer with no puff of air. Many words use this sound, so it is a good idea to practice it if you want to improve your accent.

Pivot 5: ¿Cuánto tiempo tienes_? = How long have you_?

This is used to ask someone **how long** they have been engaged in an activity or attended an event. It is also used to ask **how long** they have been in a place. It is the same as asking them **how long** they have been doing something.

Your turn! Practice using the center pivot to create numerous sentences in Spanish! Be creative by using everything you have learned in this lesson and beyond!

Pronunciation Tip: The letter 'T' regardless of where it is in the word, will not have a puff of air. The tongue stays behind the top teeth and the air stops there. Notice that *"cuánto tiempo tienes"* follows the Consonant-Vowel-Consonant pattern, so you can run them together to sound more native-like!

Expanding your Spanish:
More Key Pivot Practice

Use the *Spanish Sandwich* method (bread-meat-bread), the dressings, the key pivots, the sides, and all you know about the sounds to create your own sandwich. Also, use cognates, or words that come from the same origin, to recall words you already know. Bring these all together and make your own unique Spanish sandwiches!

¡Adelante!   *Go ahead!*

Bread:

Meat:

Bread:

Bread:

Meat:

Bread:

Bread:

Meat:

Bread:

Bread:

Meat:

Bread:

Cultural Cue: A notable difference in making friends in a Latin American country is that neighbors, or even acquaintances, are comfortable asking you about your salary, or how much you paid for your home, a car, or anything else you have purchased. While some cultures view this as an invasion of privacy, the intent is to just make conversation. If this happens, try not to be offended. There is no malice intended. It is best to share only what you are comfortable with.

Common Expressions For Small Talk

Now that you have met the neighbors, here are things you will most likely talk about.

¿Qué has hecho?	What have you been up to?
¿Cómo está la familia?	How is the family?
¿Cómo andan?	How are things?
Todo bien, no me puedo quejar.	All is well, I can't complain.
¿Tienen agua?	Do you have water?
¿Te molesta la música?	Does the music bother you?
¿Sirve el timbre?	Does the bell work?
¿Te ayudo?	Can I help you?
¿Me ayudas?	Can you help me?
Se fue la luz.	The electricity went out.
¡Qué bonita es tu casa!	How pretty your house is!
Hay mucho ruido.	There is a lot of noise.
Me encanta tu casa.	I love your house.
¿Conoces a un plomero?	Do you know a plumber?
¿Hablas Inglés?	Do you speak English?
¡Cuídate mucho!	Take good care!
¡Saludos!	Greetings!

Cultural Cue: In Latin America, respect in social interactions is most important. With the traditional family still the most common lifestyle choice, respect through proper etiquette is expected when interacting with friends or neighbors. Using the *Sandwich Spanish* model of "bread, meat, bread", you are satisfying the norms that guide social interaction. You greet, state your message, and close politely showing you are a good guest who will be accepted with open arms and a smile!

Wrap it up &
Take it To Go!

What I Can Politely Do In Native-Like Spanish:

- Make small talk with a neighbor or anyone I meet.

- Find out about their personal life and where they are from.

- Find out about their family members and their occupations.

- Find out who is going to do something.

- Use the "I" and "you" forms to speak one-on-one.

- Find out if they can help me find someone to do a job.

- What else can you do?

I Am Culturally Skilled To: Interact with others respectfully, and confidently while seeking relaxing and fun activities and using Spanish to get my needs met.

¡Gusto en saludarte!   *Nice seeing you !*

Topic Bundle 6

Let's Get Pampered

My story: getting pampered, Mayan style!

I can never forget the most unique spa experience I have ever had. I was invited by a friend to a place called El Jardín Secreto, which was a Temescal spa in the outskirts of Chihuahua. I didn't have any idea of what to expect but I went, and it was an exotic experience!

A Temescal spa treatment is similar to a sauna, where you sit in a small, enclosed hut with a pile of volcanic rocks placed in the center. Herbs are thrown onto the rocks to create a healing vapor that increases the temperature inside the hut. The intense sweat that comes with the Temescal treatment encourages blood flow and increases circulation, heart rate, and metabolic rate. Wow! This was something new, but it was amazingly relaxing and very spiritual! Afterwards, the owners offered us a cold beverage and a walk around the gardens. I will never forget this time in the secret garden where I was able to experience a true Mayan tradition in the state of Chihuahua, home to the Tarahumaras, in the largest state in Mexico!

Sandwich Spanish Ingredients

Let's Get Pampered

In this chapter you are using *Sandwich Spanish* to function in a spa or salon: the typical spaces one can get spoiled or pampered for a decent price. What else is more enjoyable than having a full body massage, a facial, a mani and pedi, as well as body wraps and more. Have a taste of your spa sandwich!

The Bread: Step 1: Greeting

Politely get attention. Always begin with: **Buenos días, buenas tardes, or buenas noches**. *Notice that we only use "buenos" in the morning!*

Disculpa, discúlpame.	Excuse me.
Perdón.	Pardon me (what did you say?).
Señor.	Sir, Mr.
Señora.	Ma'am, Married woman.
Señorita.	Single woman, and if unsure.

The Meat: Step 2: Communicate Purpose

Things you would ask or say as you arrange to visit or enjoy the spa.

¿Qué incluye el paquete del spa?	What is included in the spa package?
¿Cuál esmalte de pintura usan?	What nail polish do you use?
¿Necesito una cita para las uñas?	Do I need an appointment for my nails?
¿Qué tipo de facial hacen?	What type of facials do you do?
¿Qué productos usan?	What products do you use?
¿Cuánto dura el masaje?	How long does the massage last?
¿Las masajistas tienen licencias?	Do the therapists have licenses?
Tengo alergia a las cremas.	I am allergic to the creams.
Prefiero mas presión.	I prefer more pressure.
¿Hacen maquillaje?	Do you do makeup?
¿Hacen depilación de cejas?	Do you do eyebrow waxing?
¿Ofrecen faciales?	Do you offer (do) facials?

The Bread: Step 3: Appreciate And Depart

Things you would say as you finish your spa treatment and prepare to leave.

Gracias, muy amable.	Thank you, it was very kind of you.
Gracias. Me gusto mucho.	Thank you. I liked it a lot.
Gracias, vuelvo otro dia.	Thank you, I will be back another day.
Gracias. Lo disfrute mucho.	Thank you. I enjoyed it a lot.

Sandwich Spanish Condiments

Spice up your Sandwich with these 'Condiments'!

When you are planning to enjoy any spa treatment, you will need to ask about each aspect of the service. Use these "ingredients" to help you make plans and get pampered!

Manicure y Pedicure	Manicure and Pedicure
Remojar las uñas	Soak the nails
Cortar las cutículas	Cut the cuticles
Limar las uñas	File the nails
Secar las uñas	Dry the nails
Esmalte (pintura)	Nail polish
Manicure francesa	French manicure
Secadora	The dryer
Brillo	Clear polish

Depilacion	Waxing
Cera	Wax
Bigote	Upper lip
Cejas	Eyebrows
Barbilla	Chin
Axilas	Armpits
Bikini	Bikini
Brazos	Arms
Piernas	Legs

Masaje	Massage
Cubrir	Cover
Acostar	Lie down
Boca abajo	Face down
Boca arriba	Face up
El olor	The smell
La fragancia	The fragrance
Aceite	Oil
Crema	Cream
Más fuerte	Harder
Más suave	Softer
El cuerpo	The body
La cabeza	The head
La espalda	The back
El cuello	The neck

Growing Your Sandwich Spanish

Word Wheel with Key Pivot Practice

Pivot 1: ¿Tiene paquete de___? = Do you have a package of ____?

A package can be a combination of any services and you can choose exactly what you are looking for. Always ask, as **it is a great way to save money!** You can also use it for traveling, or anywhere you are looking for a deal!

Your turn! Practice using the center pivot to create numerous sentences in Spanish! Be creative by using everything you have learned in this lesson and beyond!

Cultural Cue: In most Spanish speaking countries, both men and women regularly visit spas for grooming and aesthetic needs. Typically, focus on appearance is extremely important, so waxing, nails, hair, and spa services are common and can be found everywhere with excellent service and pricing. A pedicure is not just something done in the summer! It is common for year-around grooming.

Pivot 2: Necesito _____. = I need to _____.

Necesito can be used to ask for a service, help, or assistance. It is very useful in requesting services at home, shopping, speaking to the doctor, or anywhere you are expressing a need. It is also easy to remember as **it resembles English.**

Your turn! Practice using the center pivot to create numerous sentences in Spanish! Be creative by using everything you have learned in this lesson and beyond!

Pronunciation Tip: When you pronounce *"necesito"* the loudest syllable is the 'SI'. Be sure not to say the 'T' as an English (no puff of air), 'R' is made with the tip of the tongue behind the top teeth. The letter 'C' has three possibilities as in English:

> C before: E, I = S   E.g. *centavo, cinturón*
> C before: A, O and U = K   E.g. *Cancún, coco, and cuando*

Note: When you have two 'C's', the first one is like 'K', and second one is like 'S':
> E.g.   Collection = *Colección* - k + s (coll - ek - sion)

Pivot 3: ¿Hacen (ofrecen)_____? = Do you do (offer)____?

"Hacen" and *"ofrecen"* are used when you approach a business, and you want to know what services they offer. You can use it to ask if a service available or if they know of another place where it may. While *"ofrecen"* is more formal, you can use either one in everyday conversation.

Your turn! Practice using the center pivot to create numerous sentences in Spanish! Be creative by using everything you have learned in this lesson and beyond!

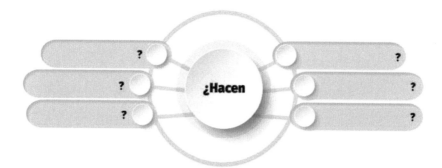

Pronunciation Tip: Remember that the 'H' is silent and C = S as it if followed by 'E'. The rule to pronounce 'C' is: C=K Before 'A', 'O' & 'U' = K= S before 'I' & 'E'.

Pivot 4: Tengo alergia a _____. = I am allergic to _____.

It is important to let personnel know if you have an allergy to anything products they use. **Be specific and up front** about anything they should know to be able to give you the best service. In this expression, *"tengo"* means "I am" but it can also mean "I have" in other contexts.

Your turn! Practice using the center pivot to create numerous sentences in Spanish! Be creative by using everything you have learned in this lesson and beyond!

> **Pronunciation Tip:** Once again, it is important to merge the "a + el" to say "al" if the word that follows is a male word. There are two 'G' sounds. In *"tengo"* the 'G' is hard because the 'G' is followed by the sound of 'O'. It is hard before, 'A', 'O', and 'U'. The second 'G' sounds in *"alergia"* is like 'H' since it is followed by 'I'. It is 'H' if it follows 'E' and 'I'.

Pivot 5: ¿Qué tipo de ____hacen? = What kind of ____ do you do?

"Qué tipo de _____ hacen" is used when we want to get more detailed information about a service before we decide to use them. This is important so that **we get what we pay for** and really want, with no misunderstandings.

Your turn! Practice using the center pivot to create numerous sentences in Spanish! Be creative by using everything you have learned in this lesson and beyond!

Pronunciation Tip: When we use *"qué"* it is pronounced as a unit of sound and sounds like "kay". In Spanish, *"qué"* has many meanings and must be understood in context to determine which one. For expressions, it means "how". For example, "¡qué bonito!" means "how beautiful!", but it means "what" in *"¿sábes qué?"* ("do you know what"?) But it is always pronounced the same. Remember, in the word "de" (of), the 'D' is like 'TH' but softer!

Expanding your Spanish:
More Key Pivot Practice

Use the *Spanish Sandwich* method (bread-meat-bread), the dressings, the key pivots, the sides, and all you know about the sounds to create your own sandwich. Also, use cognates, or words that come from the same origin, to recall words you already know. Bring these all together and make your own unique Spanish sandwiches!

¡Adelante! *Go ahead!*

Bread:

Meat:

Bread:

Bread:

Meat:

Bread:

Bread:

Meat:

Bread:

Bread:

Meat:

Bread:

Cultural Cue: Concepts of beauty differ from culture to culture. When you visit a salon or spa, try to be clear on what you would like to be sure there are no misunderstandings. For example, if you ask to wax your eyebrows, be sure you say how you want them. Do you want them thin, waxed only on the bottom, or all around? It is important to be specific so that you don't get a surprise. Once you are able to communicate this, you will be more comfortable and it will carry over to your other personal needs.

Common Spa Or Salon Expressions

Now you can garnish your *Sandwich Spanish* by using these phrases to communicate in any spa or salon setting. Use what you know about the vowels and consonants to sound like a native! Use them whenever you can!

Me gustaría hacer una cita.	I would like to make an appointment.
Prefiero un masaje con una mujer.	I would prefer a female therapist.
¿Tienen aceite de coco?	Do you have coconut oil?
¿Puede bajar la música por favor?	Can you lower the music please?
¿A qué hora abren mañana?	What time do you open tomorrow?
¿Me da más presión por favor?	Can you use more pressure please?
¿Me da menos presión por favor?	Can you use less pressure please?
Me gustaría manicure con gel.	I would like a gel manicure.
¿Puede limpiar las cejas por favor?	Can you clean up my eyebrows please?
Tengo frio/calor.	I am cold/warm.
¿Hacen uñas acrílicas aquí?	Do you do acrylic nails here?
¿Está Patricia hoy?	Is Patricia working today?

Cultural Cue: Although it is always better to call or drop in to make an appointment ahead of time, dropping in to a salon or spa is still quite common. You may have to wait, but remember that in Spanish speaking countries, time is flexible and people generally do not mind waiting for good service. If you know that this may not work for you, then stick to making appointments which means you still may have to wait a short while, but it is always worth it!

Wrap it up &
Take it To Go!

What I Can Politely Do In Native-Like Spanish:

- Make an appointment at a spa.

- Request a service that I want.

- Ask if they offer a particular service.

- Ask what kind of products are used at the spa.

- Let them know if I have any allergies to products.

- What else can you do?

I Am Culturally Skilled To: Interact with others respectfully and confidently at a spa or salon, including those who serve me, as well as those I may meet.

¡Fue un gusto servirle!
It was a pleasure serving you

Topic Bundle 7

Taxi, Taxi!

My story: getting around

Driving in Mexico can be tricky, so taking a taxi is usually your best bet. Once, when I was taking a taxi to our favorite beach club I asked the driver how much, and it was just too much! So, he said, "If you walk, it is free," then he sped off! This was the first time we saw a driver prefer to give up a fare and earn nothing, rather than negotiate a fair price! We laughed and began to walk, getting picked up soon by a more pleasant and reasonable driver! We all had a laugh that day! I guess there's always a first time!

Sandwich Spanish Ingredients

Taxi! Taxi!

In this chapter, we are using *Sandwich Spanish* to learn how to get around by taxi service. What is more pleasurable and satisfying than learning to speak Spanish so that you can go anywhere you like and feel confident that you are safe and not taken advantage of. Let's taste a piece of your sandwich.

The Bread - Step 1: Greeting

Politely get attention. Always begin with: *Buenos días, buenas tardes,* or *buenas noches.* Notice that we only use *"buenos"* in the morning!

¿Buenos días, qué tal?	Good day how are things?
Hola, ¿qué onda, cómo estás?	Hello, what's up, how are things?
Buen día. ¿Cómo le va?	Good day. How's it going?
Hola señor.	Hello sir.
Bonito día, señor.	It's a beautiful day, sir.

The Meat - Step 2: Communicate Purpose

Things you would ask or say when taking a taxi.

¿Me puede recoger?	Can you pick me up?
¿Cuánto cobra al centro?	How much do you charge to downtown?
¿Permiten perros en el taxi?	Do you allow dogs in your taxi?
Soy residente.	I am a resident. (now living here)
Soy local.	I am a local. (from this place)
¿Me permite su identificación?	May I see your I.D?
¿Me puede esperar?	Can you wait for me?
¿Dónde está el sitio de carros?	Where is the taxi stand?
¿Aceptan tarjeta?	Do you accept credit or debit cards?
Aquí está su propina.	Here is your tip.
¿Está disponible?	Are you available?

The Bread – Step 3: Appreciate And Depart

Things you would say as you prepare to leave the taxi.

Bueno, muchas gracias.	Ok, thank you very much.
Gracias, muy amable.	Thank you, you are very kind.
Bueno día. Que le vaya bien.	Have a great day. May it all go well.

Sandwich Spanish Condiments

Spice up your Sandwich with these 'Condiments'!

El chofer	The driver
El conductor	The driver (a bus)
El asiento de atrás	The back seat
El asiento de adelante	The front seat
Carro de sitio	Taxi for the area
Cambio de turno	Change of shift
Abrir la puerta	Open the door
Cerrar la puerta	Close the door
Sentar en frente	Sit in the front
Sentar atrás	Sit in the back
La cajuela	The trunk of the car (Mexico)
Señalar al taxi	Wave a taxi
Tomar un taxi	Take a taxi
Pagar el taxista (chofer)	Pay the driver
La parada	The stop (bus stop, taxi stop)
La dirección	The address
¿Me lleva ____?	Can you take me to ____?
El cambio	The change
Me recoje ____	Pick me up at ____
Me deja ____	Drop me off at ____
Adelante	Just ahead

How To Use "Me"

Something is done to you or for you

In Spanish it is important to put "me" before the action word if you want someone to do something for you.

¿Me ayudas?	Can you help me?	Will you help me?
¿Me hablas?	Can you call me?	Will you call me?

Here are the only two forms you need to say, "pick me up" and "drop me off".

¿Me recoges en la esquina?	Can you pick me up on the corner?
¿Me dejas en la esquina?	Can you drop me off at the corner?

"Lleva" has many meanings in Spanish

For this bundle we use it as "take". *"Me lleva"* is the polite way to ask the driver to take you to your destination and drop you off:

¿Me lleva al centro?	Can you take me downtown?
¿Me lleva al aeropuerto?	Can you take me to the airport?

You can also say:

¿Me deja en el centro?	Can you leave me off downtown?
¿Me deja mas adelante?	Can you leave me off further ahead?

"Me Puede + action word: Are you able to _____ for me?

When you want to ask someone if they can help you, you can use *"me puede"* and add any action word you may need.

¿Me puede hacer una cita?	Can you make an appointment for me?
¿Me puede ayudar hoy?	Can you help me today?
¿Me puede llevar a casa?	Can you take me home?

Growing Your Sandwich Spanish

Word Wheel with Key Pivot Practice

Pivot 1: ¿Me llevas a (al) ___? = Can you take me to ___?

"Me llevas" can be used to ask someone to take you somewhere by car or taxi. It is used to make a request to get to a destination. Remember that double 'LL' is pronounced like 'Y' and the vowels are pure! E = A, and 'A' is like "father".

Your turn! Practice using the center pivot to create numerous sentences in Spanish! Be creative by using everything you have learned in this lesson and beyond!

> **Cultural Cue:** Many people feel it is not necessary to tip cab drivers, but when they provide a great service or help you with your luggage, it is a good idea to tip them. They may even make a special trip, make an extra stop, or help you find something. So, for any extra service, it is always a good idea to tip. It is always appreciated!

Pivot 2: ¿Me puede _____? = Can you _____?

"Me puede" refers to asking someone if they are willing and able to do something for you. It is ALWAYS followed by an action word in its natural form. If you're **asking a favor**, this is the correct form to use.

Your turn! Practice using the center pivot to create numerous sentences in Spanish! Be creative by using everything you have learned in this lesson and beyond!

Pronunciation Tip: The sound of 'E' is always a long 'A' as in "ate". Be sure that both sounds are the same and each has the same value. With only five vowels to learn, you can always rely on them to be the same sound, pure and without a long puff of air! Just short and sweet!

Pivot 3: ¿Está disponible _____? = Are you available _____?

"Está disponible" can be followed by a time, or you can add "to" with an action word: "Are you available to help me?" You can also ask if someone is available at a certain time, or for a duration of time.

Your turn! Practice using the center pivot to create numerous sentences in Spanish! Be creative by using everything you have learned in this lesson and beyond!

Pronunciation Tip: Remember! Go back to the five pure vowels and the 12 exceptions so that your pronunciation will be clear and native-like! You will feel more confident to speak and improve your skills if you can get close to those sounds! Also, the 'D' in *"disponible"* is like 'TH' so be sure to bite your tongue when you begin the word, just a little!

Pivot 4: ¿Me recoge _____? = ¿Can you pick me up _____?

"Me recoge" is used to ask someone for a ride, or a fare if it is a taxi or hired car. It is used before the place you want to be picked up from, or before a specific time you would like to be picked up.

Your turn! Practice using the center pivot to create numerous sentences in Spanish! Be creative by using everything you have learned in this lesson and beyond!

Pronunciation Tip: The sound of 'G' in Spanish is pronounced as a moderate 'H' sound. It is neither far back in the throat nor is it soft, as in the English 'H'. The 'R' at the beginning of the word is strong, so imagine that it is two 'R's'. If you bring your tongue from the back of your mouth to the front so that it softly taps above the back of your teeth, you will have it!

Pivot 5: Aquí está el/la _____. = Here is the _____.

You can use *"aquí está"*, if you are looking for something and you find it, or if you want to give or hand something to someone. It is also used to locate things and make their location known to others. Alone, *"aquí está"* means "here it is." This can be a stand-alone sentence. It is like saying "I found it".

Your turn! Practice using the center pivot to create numerous sentences in Spanish! Be creative by using everything you have learned in this lesson and beyond!

> **Pronunciation Tip:** *"Aquí"* is pronounced like "a key" and is the 12th exception to speaking Spanish phonetically. The combination of the 'U' and 'I' together combine to sound like long 'E', as in "cheat". It means "here".

Expanding your Spanish:
More Key Pivot Practice

Use the *Spanish Sandwich* method (bread-meat-bread), the dressings, the key pivots, the sides, and all you know about the sounds to create your own sandwich. Also, use cognates, or words that come from the same origin, to recall words you already know. Bring these all together and make your own unique Spanish sandwiches!

¡Adelante!   *Go ahead!*

Bread:

Meat:

Bread:

Bread:

Meat:

Bread:

Bread:

Meat:

Bread:

Bread:

Meat:

Bread:

Cultural Cue: Uber and other similar services are expanding rapidly across Mexico and Latin America. However, it is still a good idea to plan to pay cash in the local currency for taxis. Most drivers *"choferes"* know some English, and some can even speak their own local indigenous language. So, it is a good idea to be ready to tell them in Spanish where you're heading or have it written down, and they will get you to your destination, safe and sound.

Common Expressions For Taking A Taxi

Now you can garnish your *Sandwich Spanish* by using these phrases to communicate when traveling by taxi. Use what you know about the vowels and consonants to sound like a native! Use them whenever you can!

¿Qué tan lejos esta?	How far is it?
¿Tiene cambio?	Do you have change?
¿Puede manejar más despacio?	Can you drive a bit slower?
¿Eres de aquí?	Are you from here?
¿Cobras por persona?	Do you charge per person?
¿Aceptas dólares?	Do you accept dollars?
¿A cuánto aceptas dólares?	At what rate do you accept dollars?
¿Conoces un doctor cerca?	Do you know any doctors nearby?
Estoy apurado (a).	I am in a hurry.
¿Vámos a llegar a tiempo?	Are we going to arrive on time?
¿Dónde puedo comprar dólares?	Where can I buy dollars?
¿Hoy es un día de festivo?	Is today a holiday?
¿Me puede esperar?	Can you wait for me?
¿Cuánto tarda en llegar?	How long does it take to get there?
¿Hay mucho tráfico?	Is there much traffic?
¿Me ayuda con mis maletas?	Will you help me with my luggage?

Wrap it up &
Take it To Go!

What I Can Politely Do In Native-Like Spanish:

- I can make small talk with the taxi driver.

- I can order a taxi by phone.

- I can find out how long and how far a destination is.

- I can express where to pick me up and drop me off.

- I find out if they allow dogs in their taxis.

- I can ask someone if they can do something for me.

- I can find out if a driver is available.

- What else can you do?

I AM CULTURALLY SKILLED TO: Interact with others respectfully and confidently while traveling by taxi using Spanish to get my needs met.

¡ Buen chofer!	*Great driver!*
¡ Muy buen servicio!	*Very good service*

Topic Bundle 8

Talk to the Handyman

My story: Max and his magical Chevy

One thing's for sure, a Mexican handyman is like no other! They can fix anything, or at least bring one of their "compadres" who can! Max, my handyman, was doing various jobs around the house. In the meantime, I was looking for someone to reupholster six dining room chairs. He had a friend with a shop, so we arranged for him to do the job. When it was time to take the chairs, I asked him if he had a truck as I knew he only had a small, compact Chevy. Of course, he said, "don't worry, everything fits in a Chevy!" Sure enough, he was able to get the six large chairs into that car (just like a clown car)! I am not sure how, but when they were done, he delivered them to me, in the Chevy, in perfect condition! All six at once! I still do not know how they all fit, but he did it! Long live the power of positive thinking! I have always said, Mexicans can fix anything, or at least their compadre can!

Sandwich Spanish Ingredients

Talk to the Handyman

In this chapter, we are using *Sandwich Spanish* to interact and converse with handymen who install or repair things in our home. Learning to express your needs, understanding what they will do, and how much it will cost is key to being satisfied with the work. What is more pleasurable and satisfying than learning to speak Spanish so that you can get things done at home without asking for a translator or risking a misunderstanding! Let's taste a piece of your sandwich.

THE BREAD- STEP 1: Greeting

Politely get attention. Always begin with: *Buenos días, buenas tardes,* or *buenas noches.* Notice that we only use *"buenos"* in the morning!

¿Buenos días, qué tal?	Good morning, how are things?
¿Hola, qué onda? ¿Cómo le va?	Hi, what's up? How are things?
Buen día. ¿Qué dices?	Good day. What do you say?

THE MEAT - STEP 2: Communicate purpose

Things you would ask or tell the handyman.

Tengo problemas con la plomería.	I have problems with the plumbing.
Hay una fuga abajo del lavabo.	There's a leak under the sink.
¿Qué tiene el calentador de agua?	What is wrong with the hot water tank?
¿Puedes revisar los aires?	Can you check the air conditioners?
No funciona la secadora.	The dryer doesn't work.
Los abanicos no prenden.	The fans won't turn on.
¿Qué materiales necesitas?	What materials (parts) do you need?
¿Cuánto cobras el trabajo?	How much do you charge for this job?
¿Cuándo terminas?	When will you finish?
¿Hay garantía para el trabajo?	Is there a warranty on this job?
¿Me da un recibo?	Can you give me a receipt?

THE BREAD : STEP 3: Appreciate and depart

Things you would say as you finish your interaction.

Bueno. Bien hecho.	Okay. Well done.
Buen trabajo. Gracias.	Good job. Thank you.
Gracias. Te espero mañana.	Thank you. I will expect you tomorrow.

Sandwich Spanish Condiments

Spice up your Sandwich with these 'Condiments'!

Plumbing: The sink, tub, toilet, washer, hot water tank (boiler):

Plomero o fontanero	The plumber
La regadera	The shower
El lavabo de la cocina	The kitchen sink
La tubería	The pipes
La tina del baño	The bathtub
La tasa del baño	The toilet
La fuga	The leak
Arréglalo	Fix it
Descompone	Breaks down
Las llaves	The faucet
El drenaje	The drain (drainage)
La bomba del agua	The water pump
El boiler	The hot water tank
La cisterna	The water reserve (in the ground)
El tinaco	The water tank (on top of the roof)

Electricity: The lights, air conditioner, plugs, and appliances

Electricista	Electrician
La luz	The light
El foco	The light bulb
El interruptor	The light switch
El enchufe	The light socket
Le conexión	The connection
El aire	The air conditioner
El abanico	The fan
Instalar	Install
Agua o gas	Water or gas
El corriente	The current (electric)
El calentón	The heater
La reparación	Repair
Conectar	To connect (the stove, the refrigerator)
El trabajo	The job
La garantía	Warranty
El pago	The payment

Cultural Cue: *"El mil usos"* is the "Jack of all trades". It is the term used for a handyman who has experience fixing just about anything in your home. In Mexico, this is true! They can usually find a solution to your problem. If they can't, they always know someone, *"el compadre"* who can do the job, and do it well!

How To Talk About A Household Challenge

There are various ways to let someone know that something is just not working or not working right. While it can be used to talk about household appliances, electrical issues, and plumbing challenges, these can also be used to talk about how things in general are not working.

Problem/challenge: "It is not working", or "it doesn't work." They all mean the same and all of them are correct.

No jala	It does not work
No funciona	It does not work
No sirve	It does not work
No prende	It does not turn on (start)
No trabaja	It does not work

If it is working, but not perfectly.

Trabaja, pero no está bien	It is working, but something is just not right.

¿Qué tipo de trabajo haces?	What type of work do you do?
Soy carpintero.	I am a carpenter.
Hago carpintería.	I do carpentry.
Hago clósets y muebles.	I make closets and furniture.
Hago gabinetes de cocina.	I make kitchen cabinets.
Soy electricista.	I am an electrician.
Instalo secadoras y luces.	I install clothes dryers and lighting.
Arreglo todo lo eléctrico.	I fix everything that is electric.
Soy pintor.	I am a painter.
Pinto paredes.	I paint walls.
Pinto muebles y muros también.	I paint furniture and walls too.
Soy plomero (fontanero).	I am a plumber.

Arreglo regaderas.	I fix showers.
Instalo bombas de agua.	I install water pumps.
Instalo calentadores de agua.	I install water heaters (boilers).
Instalo llaves del baño y cocina.	I install bathroom and kitchen faucets.
Soy albañil.	I am a brick layer.
Pongo pisos de cerámica	I install ceramic flooring.
Construyo bardas y patios.	I build outside walls and patios.
Instalo azulejo en el baño.	I install bathroom tiles.

Growing Your Sandwich Spanish

Word Wheel with Key Pivot Practice

Pivot 1: ¿Sábes arreglar el (la) __? = Do you know how to fix a __?

The phrase *"sábes arreglar el (la) _____"* means "do you know how to fix" something. In this case, *"sábes"* means "do you know how". It is one word in Spanish that means four in English! You can add any action word to ask someone if they know how to do something. In this case, we are asking if they know how to fix something.

Your turn! Practice using the center pivot to create numerous sentences in Spanish! Be creative by using everything you have learned in this lesson and beyond!

> **Cultural Cue:** Remember that time is a continuum in some countries so if someone is not on time, it does not mean they cannot do a great job for a fair price. They may be taking public transportation or traveling a long distance. Try to be patient and you will be happy with the results. Be sure to settle the price before the job is done, preferably in writing before the work begins. In Spanish they say *"lo barato te puede salir caro."* In other words, cheap can cost you more in the end.

Pivot 2: ¿Puede revisar el (la) ___? = Can you check out the ___?

This phrase can be used to ask someone to check or review anything you are not sure of. In a general sense, it can be used to check out a job you did, your writing, something you cooked, your car, etc.

Your turn! Practice using the center pivot to create numerous sentences in Spanish! Be creative by using everything you have learned in this lesson and beyond!

Pronunciation Tip: It is important to remember that the 'V' in *"revisar"* is almost a 'B' and you should feel your lips vibrate as you say the word. Try not to bite your tongue but bring your lips together instead. For your accent to be native-like, you must also remember that the 'D' in *"puede"* is pronounced as 'TH'. The difference in these two sounds of English and Spanish is one of the most important distinctions necessary to take away your gringo accent.

Pivot 3: ¿Qué tiene _____? = What is wrong with _____?

The phrase *"qué tiene"* is used when you feel or sense that something is wrong. It can be a machine, a person, an animal, etc. Idiomatically it is like saying, "what is up with this thing?" "What's going on?"

Your turn! Practice using the center pivot to create numerous sentences in Spanish! Be creative by using everything you have learned in this lesson and beyond!

Pronunciation Tip: Once again, remember that in Spanish, the 'T' sound at the beginning of a word like *"tiene"*, has no puff of air as 'T' does in English. Another reminder is that *"que"* is pronounced "KAY" and is a word with multiple meanings but is always spelled the same.

Pivot 4: El (la) _____ no prende. = The _____ does not turn on.

When a machine, a car, a lamp, a computer, or anything that runs on electricity does not turn on, we say *"no prende."* This means "it won't turn on" or "there is no current". It can also be used for a burner, a hot water tank (boiler) or any other apparatus that uses gas or any other kind of fuel. You can use *"no prende"* alone without specifying what thing.

Your turn! Practice using the center pivot to create numerous sentences in Spanish! Be creative by using everything you have learned in this lesson and beyond!

Pronunciation Tip: You learned that Spanish is a consonant, vowel, consonant vowel language. This means that if you don't breathe between words you'll sound more native-like. The 'R' in *prende* is made with the tapping of the of the tongue on the backside of your upper teeth. *"No prende"* can be pronounced as if it were one word, giving you the rhythm of Spanish needed to sound native-like. When you put it all together, it will add to improving your overall accent in spoken Spanish.

Pivot 5: Tengo problemas con __. = I am having trouble with ___.

The phrase *"tengo problemas con"* can be used in a variety of situations including talking about people, things, concepts, and health. It means that you know something is not right, but you need help in finding out exactly what is wrong. It is possible to use *"tengo problemas"* alone to mean "I have problems".

Your turn! Practice using the center pivot to create numerous sentences in Spanish! Be creative by using everything you have learned in this lesson and beyond!

> **Pronunciation Tip:** Going back to the pure vowels, we look at the word *"con"* that looks like "con man" in English. However, it is pronounced as a long 'O' as in "ice cream CONE". Using "cone" instead of *"con"* will greatly improve your accent. Pronouncing all five vowels correctly also will, since they are frequently used when we Speak Spanish. You are getting close to native-like Spanish!

Expanding your Spanish: More Key Pivot Practice

Create your own **Spanish Sandwiches**: be creative using the **Sandwich Ingredients** and **Word Wheel Pivots.** You already know a lot of words in Spanish! Cognates are words in both languages that come from the same origin. Use them to complete your Sandwiches!

¡Adelante! *Go ahead!*

Bread:

Meat:

Bread:

Bread:

Meat:

Bread:

Bread:

Meat:

Bread:

Bread:

Meat:

Bread:

Cultural Cue: When having work done in your home by individual service personnel, it is a good idea to prepare to pay them in cash in the local currency as it is more convenient for them this way. It is still important to get an invoice or receipt with the guarantee included, just in case you need to call them back. If you have hired a contractor, you may be able to pay via debit or credit card, PayPal, or other online means. Most workers use WhatsApp to set up appointments and keep you posted of their arrival times and any follow-up communication, so be sure to download the app.

Common Expressions For The Handyman

Now you can garnish your *Sandwich Spanish* by using these phrases to communicate when interacting with a handy man. Use what you know about pronouncing the vowels and consonants to sound like a native!

¿Me arregla _____?	Can you fix the _____?
Esta descompuesto el (la) _____.	The_____ is not working.
No sirve el (la)_____.	The _____ doesn't work.
No funciona el (la) _____.	The _____ doesn't work.
Funciona bien.	It works fine.
Algo le falta.	Something is missing.
¿Cuándo puedes venir?	When can you come?
¿Cuánto cobras?	How much do you charge?
¿Cuándo vienes?	When are you coming?
¿Cuánto cuesta el material?	How much are the parts/materials.
¿Tiene garantía?	Does it have a guarantee?
¿Necesitas algo?	Do you need anything?
¿Apago el cortacircuitos (breaker)?	Should I shut off the circuit breaker?
¿La conexión está segura?	Is the connection safe?
¿Está instalada?	Is it installed?
¿Está listo?	Is it done? Is it ready to go?
Hace ruido.	It makes noise.
¿Tiene control remoto?	Does it have a remote control?
¡Quedó bien!	It turned out well!
¡Salió bien!	It turned out well!
¿Va a regresar mañana?	Will you be back tomorrow?
Lo barato te puede salir caro.	Cheap can cost more in the end.
¡Es muy servicial!	He is very helpful.
¡Mucho ojo!	Be careful!
¡Con cuidado!	Be careful!
Te espero a la una.	I will wait for you at 1:00pm.

Wrap it up &
Take it To Go!

What I Can Politely Do In Native-Like Spanish:

- I can tell the handyman what the problem is.

- I can make an appointment with a handyman.

- I can ask about cost and materials.

- I can complement the handyman on his work.

- I can ask about a warranty for the job.

- I can ask about safety.

- What else can you do?

I AM CULTURALLY SKILLED TO: Interact with service personnel respectfully and confidently to solve problems in my home and getting my needs met.

¡ Haces buen trabajo!   *You do great work!*

Your Own Journey Has Begun!

You did it! You have successfully navigated 40 Spanish pivots or high-frequency expressions, while using many, many known and new words to communicate in everyday Spanish! You can deliver a message and get your needs met! You have learned common, useful expressions to use in a restaurant, hotel, resort, bus or train station, spa, with neighbors, the handyman, or in a taxi! You can find entertainment wherever you go, and you can even get things done around the house with your favorite handyman.

Most of all, using your *Sandwich Spanish*, you know the importance of cultural appropriateness by greeting everyone pleasantly, adding your purpose for approaching them, and closing your interaction with a Spanish pleasantry. With all of this, you have come much closer to becoming a Spanish speaker. You are on the road to fulfilling a lifetime goal, with a strong foundation to build upon.

Over time, as you continue on your journey to becoming a Spanish speaker, you will create your own stories that center around your unique experiences learning spoken Spanish. Surely, there will be many tales to tell that describe the outcome of your efforts to communicate in various settings in the community. Some will make you laugh for a long time after, but they make for great stories.

Talking with native speakers and interacting in everyday activities will give you the chance to use what you've learned in *Sandwich Spanish*. Take advantage of every opportunity to practice: it is the only road to improving your language skills! Watch movies, listen to music, and stay engaged in Spanish any way you can! Make friends who don't speak your language! But most of all, remember to stay light in your journey and have fun as you use what you have learned in *Sandwich Spanish*.

As you document your stories, you too will look back fondly on the fun, and humorous events that are bound to take place, and the memorable people you will meet as you try out your new language!

So, the next time someone asks you if you speak Spanish, you can smile and say, *"sí, hablo Español"*!

¡Bien hecho! Well done!

¡Felicidades! Congratulations!

List of 40 Sandwich Spanish Pivots

Topic Bundle 1: Visiting a Restaurant

1. Me gustaría _____.	I would like (to)_____.
2. ¿Tiene_____?	Do you/he/she/it have _____.
3. ¿Dónde esta _____?	Where is _____?
4. Tráigame _____.	Bring me _____.
5. Me trae_____.	Bring me _____.

Topic Bundle 2: Traveling by Bus or Train

1. ¿Hay_____? Hay_____.	Is there? Are there? There is. There are.
2. ¿Cuánto cuesta?	How much does it cost?
3. Me gustaría pagar_____.	I would like to pay _____.
4. ¿Me da_____?	Can you give me _____?
5. ¿A qué hora sale_____?	At what time does _____ leave?

Topic Bundle 3: Hotel and Resort

1. Prefiero _____.	I prefer _____.
2. ¿Tienen _____?	Do you carry (sell) _____?
3. ¿Cobran _____?	Do you charge _____?
4. ¿Podemos _____?	Can we _____?
5. ¿Es posible _____?	Is it possible (to) _____?

Topic Bundle 4: Entertainment and Fun

1. Vamos a _____.	Let's _____.
2. ¿Dónde hay _____?	Where is (are) there _____?
3. ¿Incluye _____?	Does it (the price) include _____?
4. ¿Quién va a _____?	Who is going to _____?
5. ¿Cuánto cobran _____?	How much do they (you) charge for _____?

Topic Bundle 5: Socializing with Neighbors

1. Soy.	I am _____ (permanent condition).
2. Eres.	You are _____(permanent condition).
3. ¿Sabes de _____?	Do you know of (a) any _____?
4. ¿Tienes _____?	Do you have _____?
5. ¿Cuánto tiempo tienes _____?	How long have you been _____?

Topic Bundle 6: Let's Get Pampered!

1. ¿Tienen paquete de? _____?	Do you have packages for _____?
2. Necesito _____.	I need _____.
3. ¿Hacen _____?	Do you do _____?
4. Tengo alergia (a) _____.	I am allergic to _____.
5. ¿Qué tipo de _____ hacen?	What type of _____do you do (offer)?

Topic Bundle 7: ¡Taxi, Taxi!

1. ¿Me llevas a _____?	Can you take me to _____.
2. ¿Me puede _____?	Can you _____?
3. ¿Está disponible?	Are you (is it) available?
4. ¿Me recoge _____?	Can you pick me up _____?
5. Aquí esta.	Here it is.

Topic Bundle 8: Talk to the Handyman

1. ¿Sabes arreglar _____?	Do you know how to fix _____?
2. ¿Puede revisar _____?	Can you check _____?
3. ¿Qué tiene _____?	What is wrong with _____?
4. No prende.	It won't turn on. It does not work.
5. Tengo problemas con _____.	I have problems with _____.

Online Resources for Supporting Your Sandwich Spanish

Here is a list of some useful online sites that were selected to support what you have learned about the topic bundles in *Sandwich Spanish*. There are so many more resources online including podcasts, websites, youtube, Instagram,etc. Everything helps and adds to your journey to becoming bilingual!

http://www.spanishdict.com/phrases/eat

https://itsnachotime.com/ordering-food/

www.whynotspanish.com

https://takelessons.com/blog/cognates-in-Spanish-z03

https://www.youtube.com/channel/UCxsmrNI05NHuHCsNe8UhJ3w

https://www.theguardian.com/travel/2009/jul/07/learn-spanish-phrases-restaurant

https://spanishlandschool.com/spanish-phrases-for-travelers/

https://www.fluentu.com/blog/spanish/useful-spanish-travel-phrases-words/

Taking a taxi:
https://www.youtube.com/watch?v=5UMowhO3d5Q

https://www.butterflyspanish.com/
This blog provides information on the 10 best non-traditional websites for learning Spanish online including TV such as Telemundo and Univision:

https://www.fluentu.com/blog/spanish/best-websites-to-learn-spanish/

Excellent resource for 25 reasons to learn Spanish:
https://www.realfastspanish.com/motivation/25-reasons-learn-spanish

10 Things to know:
https://www.oyster.com/articles/47238-10-things-every-traveler-should-know-before-going-to-mexico/

My Bilingual Journey in Pictures

Abdelli, Batroun, North Lebanon

Uniontown, PA. My home town

*Xinantecatl Volcanoe, Toluca
Estado de Mexico, Mexico*

Chihuahua, Chihuahua, Mexico,

*University of Buffalo, Amherst, New York.
Graduate School of Education*

Riviera Maya, Playa del Carmen, Quintana Roo